The Chartered Management Institute

chartered
management
institute

inspiring leaders

The Chartered Management Institute is the only chartered professional body that is dedicated to management and leadership. We are committed to raising the performance of business by championing management.

We represent 71,000 individual managers and have 450 corporate members. Within the Institute there are also a number of distinct specialisms, including the Institute of Business Consulting and Women in Management Network.

We exist to help managers tackle the management challenges they face on a daily basis by raising the standard of management in the UK. We are here to help individuals become better managers and companies develop better managers.

We do this through a wide range of products and services, from practical management checklists to tailored training and qualifications. We produce research on the latest 'hot' management issues, provide a vast array of useful information through our online management information centre, as well as offering consultancy services and career information.

You can access these resources 'off the shelf' or we can provide solutions just for you. Our range of products and services is designed to ensure companies and managers develop their potential and excel. Whether you are at the start of your career or a proven performer in the boardroom, we have something for you.

We engage policy makers and opinion formers and, as the leading authority on management, we are regularly consulted on a range of management issues. Through our in-depth research and regular policy surveys of members, we have a deep understanding of the latest management trends.

For more information visit our website **www.managers.org.uk** or call us on **01536 207307**.

Chartered Manager

chartered
management
institute
inspiring leaders

Transform the way you work

The Chartered Management Institute's Chartered Manager award is the ultimate accolade for practising professional managers. Designed to transform the way you think about your work and how you add value to your organisation, it is based on demonstrating measurable impact.

This unique award proves your ability to make a real difference in the workplace.

Chartered Manager focuses on the six vital business skills of:

- Leading people
- Managing change
- Meeting customer needs
- Managing information and knowledge
- Managing activities and resources
- Managing yourself

Transform your organisation

There is a clear and well-established link between good management and improved organisational performance. Recognising this, the Chartered Manager scheme requires individuals to demonstrate how they are applying their leadership and change management skills to make significant impact within their organisation.

Transform your career

Whatever career stage a manager is at Chartered Manager will set them apart. Chartered Manager has proven to be a stimulus to career progression, either via recognition by their current employer or through the motivation to move on to more challenging roles with new employers.

But don't take just our word for it ...
Chartered Manager has transformed the careers and organisations of managers in all sectors.

- *'Being a Chartered Manager was one of the main contributing factors which led to my recent promotion.'*
Lloyd Ross, Programme Delivery Manager, British Nuclear Fuels

- *'I am quite sure that a part of the reason for my success in achieving my appointment was due to my Chartered Manager award which provided excellent, independent evidence that I was a high quality manager.'*
Donaree Marshall, Head of Programme Management Office, Water Service, Belfast

- *'The whole process has been very positive, giving me confidence in my strengths as a manager but also helping me to identify the areas of my skills that I want to develop. I am delighted and proud to have the accolade of Chartered Manager.'*
Allen Hudson, School Support Services Manager, Dudley Metropolitan County Council

- *'As we are in a time of profound change, I believe that I have, as a result of my change management skills, been able to provide leadership to my staff. Indeed, I took over three teams and carefully built an integrated team, which is beginning to perform really well. I believe that the process I went through to gain Chartered Manager status assisted me in achieving this and consequently was of considerable benefit to my organisation.'*
George Smart, SPO and D/Head of Resettlement, HM Prison Swaleside

To find out more or to request further information please visit our website **www.managers.org.uk/cmgr** or call us on **01536 207429**.

Contents

CHAPTER 02

CHAPTER 03

CHAPTER 04

WHY IS CASH AND THE MANAGEMENT OF WORKING CAPITAL IMPORTANT?

CHAPTER 05

CHAPTER 06

CHAPTER 07

CHAPTER 08

CHAPTER 09

CHAPTER 10

Preface

Depending on how far you are willing to stretch the definition, there are well over a million non-financial managers in Britain, with countless more in other countries. Many of them need, and would like, to know more about finance. This knowledge is needed for their jobs and it seems to grow in importance year by year. There are of course a number of books for non-financial managers, some of them very good, but I firmly believe there is a call for this one too. It reflects my selection of the subjects that you will find most useful and also my interpretation of those subjects. I give my own point of view in some areas and I hope that this will be useful and thought-provoking. I am an experienced manager, as well as a speaker and writer on the topics covered and I hope that this is apparent.

I would like you to read the book from cover to cover but I realise that, probably, you will not. This may be sensible because, if you are like most managers, you are very busy and time is at a premium. To cater for this I have taken care to divide each chapter into many easily identified sections and you may want to home in on just the ones that you need.

Each chapter ends with some questions, so you can test your knowledge of the contents of that chapter. The answers are given at the end of the book. Many of the questions call for not much more than a one-word answer, but some are detailed exercises that will take quite a bit of time. What you do with the questions is your choice. You might decide to ignore them, to do just some or conscientiously to do all of them. You could of course read through the questions and answers, treating them as extensions of the chapters. No doubt you will make the decision that is right for you.

Thank you for choosing this book. I have enjoyed writing it and I hope that you enjoy reading it, or at the very least find it useful.

Roger Mason

How do the basics of finance fit together?

This opening chapter divides naturally into two distinct sections. The first gives some elementary information about accounts and finance, explains some of the terms that you will encounter and answers some questions that may be troubling you. The second section, like the rest of the book, deals with specific topics. They relate to the basics of bookkeeping, which are relevant in all businesses and the different types of account in the bookkeeping system. The chapter goes further by explaining some adjustments that are usually necessary when accounts are prepared. The topics covered are:

First section

- The need for bookkeeping, accounts and finance.
- How much should we leave to the accountants?
- Some financial terms explained.
- Answers to ten questions frequently asked by non-financial managers.

Second section

- Single entry bookkeeping.
- The concept of double entry bookkeeping.
- The basic rules and disciplines of double entry bookkeeping.
- Example of double entry bookkeeping postings.
- The different types of account.
- Trial balance, profit statement and balance sheet.
- Accounting adjustments.

The chapter, like all the chapters in the book, ends with some questions, so you can test your understanding. The answers are at the end of the book.

First section

The need for bookkeeping, accounts and finance

Why do companies and other businesses keep financial records and use the information that they contain? I suggest that there are four main reasons:

- For the benefit of the owners.
- For the benefit of the managers.
- To comply with the law.
- To satisfy the tax authorities.

In some countries, though not generally in Britain, managers can be extremely creative with the financial records. In one European country directors are said to keep three sets of records: one for the tax authorities, one for the owners and the real one for themselves. As I hope to sell the book in that country, I will not name it. It may be an apocryphal story anyway.

What do in-house accountants do? Well if you want to annoy them, tell them that they are bean counters or score keepers. If you want to make them mad, say that they are also boring. We have John Cleese in a Monty Python sketch to thank for that particular misunderstanding. If you really want to have them foaming at the mouth, say that they are all introverts and that you can tell because they will look at your shoes rather than look you in the eye. Mind you, they are not so introverted as actuaries who reputedly look at their own shoes rather than your shoes. Writing as an accountant, I can categorically confirm that everything in this paragraph is absolutely outrageous and that there is no truth in any of it.

'Accounts Department' implies that it is the department that runs the bookkeeping system and prepares the accounts. Functions such as payroll are usually part of the accounts department. The term 'Finance' implies rather wider functions, incorporating such things as 'Treasury'.

Obviously the records are kept in financial terms. In some businesses the accounts or finance departments do not go much beyond the basic records needed to comply with the law, the demands of the tax authorities and the requirement to prepare the statutory accounts. Most businesses go considerably further and, in these, accounts and finance are dynamically involved in helping the managers run the business. This book caters for non-financial managers in these more dynamic businesses and other non-financial managers who would like to know more.

How much should we leave to the accountants?

It is possible to make a case for non-financial managers leaving nearly everything financial to the specialist accountants. Such a case would probably have three main planks:

1. It is a matter of dispute, but management theory about division of labour indicates that profits are maximised if people specialise and do what they are trained to do. Henry Ford did not get rich by making the women who sewed seat covers for his cars fit the rear axles as well.

2. People generally do best if they enjoy their work. I have certainly found this to be true and fortunately I enjoy speaking and writing. Quite a few non-financial managers do not enjoy finance.

3. Working with finance takes time and it is time taken away from the job that non-financial managers are primarily employed to do. If, for example, a sales manager spends three hours a week on finance, then that is three hours a week less time available in which to make sales. Businesses need sales and it does matter.

Although these arguments have some validity, you would expect the writer of this book to reject them, which I do. There are a lot of good reasons why non-financial managers should have some knowledge of finance and make a contribution in financial matters. For a start, modern thinking is in some respects moving away from the division of labour, and workers may well be multi-skilled. Many of Henry Ford's managers very probably had secretaries to do their typing, but most of today's equivalents are expected to look after their own emails. It is more true than ever that managers need information to manage effectively and, inevitably, quite a bit of this information will be financial information. Managers are at a disadvantage if they do not have sufficient knowledge at least to cope with it.

Managers who thoroughly understand the matter in hand are often best placed to contribute effectively to financial decisions, and often such managers are non-financial managers. Be that as it may, a financial role is often forced on non-financial managers. For example, headmasters are routinely forced to be involved in the financial management of their schools, and senior doctors and nurses are routinely expected to be involved in the financial management of their hospitals. Woe betide them if they do not get involved, or cannot do it properly. Their schools and hospitals will probably suffer and so will they.

Accountants need your help in order to help you. Despite doing their best for you (or not, as the case may be), they may not be able to give you what you want and need unless you are able to communicate effectively with them. Finally, there is a continuing need for capable and well-rounded chief executives, and it goes without saying that such people must have some knowledge of finance. Non-financial managers must, or at least should, fill many of these positions. Some people believe that there are more than enough accountants in these jobs now. This is of course unfair to accountants, but as an accountant myself I can just about get away with reporting the view.

There really is not much of a case to answer. Non-financial managers are making a mistake if they leave it all to the accountants.

Some financial terms explained

Perhaps you are surrounded by accountants who talk to each other, and perhaps to you, too, using terms with which you are not familiar. Even worse, perhaps your non-financial colleagues appear to understand them, though of course they might be bluffing. I will try to help at the start of this book by listing some of the commonly used terms and nailing exactly what they mean.

Accrual	This is an expense incurred but not yet entered into the double entry bookkeeping system. Details are in this chapter.
Bad debt	This is money owing by a customer, which either the customer cannot pay or which the customer will not pay and you are unwilling to take steps to force payment. Details are in Chapter 10.
Breakeven point	This occurs at the level of sales where the costs (fixed and variable) exactly equal the revenue. Details are in Chapter 8.
Cash	This is usually taken to mean the total of the bank balances plus notes and coins in the petty cash box. It can be, and very often is, a negative figure. Details are in Chapter 4.
Current assets	These are assets intended for use in a short period, usually taken to be less than a year. Details are in Chapter 2.
Current liabilities	These are liabilities which must be discharged in the short term, usually taken to be less than a year. Details are in Chapter 2.

Depreciation

This is the part of the cost of a fixed asset (which is held for the long term) which is released as an expense into the profit and loss account in a single period. Details are in this chapter.

Discounted cash flow

This measures the expected profitability of a project, taking into account the timing of cash going out and coming in. Details are in Chapter 6.

Fixed assets

These assets are a capital investment. They will be used in the long term and will retain at least some of their value over the long term, which is usually taken to be a period longer than one year. Details are in Chapter 2.

Flexible budgets

These budgets present a range of costs to be used to accommodate a range of outcomes. Details are in Chapter 7.

Gearing

This is a ratio that compares the finance provided by banks and other lenders with the finance provided by the owners (often the shareholders). Details are given in Chapter 5.

Marginal costing

This is a system of costing that excludes fixed costs and concentrates on marginal costs. It is the change in cost which occurs when the volume of output is increased or reduced by one unit. Details are in Chapter 8.

Payback

This measures the period of time taken for an investment to recover its cost. Details are in Chapter 6.

Reserves and provisions

These are deductions in the profit and loss account to guard against contingencies that may, but will not definitely, arise. Bad debt reserve is an example. Details are in this chapter.

Revenue reserves

These are accumulated net profits, after taxation, dividends and distributions.

Return on capital employed

This is profit expressed as a percentage of the net value of the money invested in the business. Details are in Chapter 5.

Return on investment

This is the average increase in profits per year caused by an investment, expressed as a percentage of the investment. Details are in Chapter 6.

Trial balance

This is a listing of every balance in a double entry bookkeeping system. The total of the debit balances must equal the total of the credit balances. Details are in this chapter.

Standard costing

This is the setting of standards for the various elements of cost, then establishing favourable or unfavourable variances by comparing actual results

with the standards. Details are in
Chapter 8.

Working capital   This is the difference between current
assets and current liabilities. Details
are in Chapter 4.

Answers to ten questions frequently asked by non-financial managers

I am often asked questions by non-financial managers and it
seems a good idea to list ten of the most common, together with
my answers. Many of them may well be of interest to you.

We are making a good profit so how can we possibly be short of cash?

It is often said that there are some things that every generation has
to discover for itself. The fact that all women grow to be like their
mothers is one – a cause of great satisfaction in my household.
Another is that profit and cash are most definitely not the same
thing. There are numerous reasons for this. To name just three:
dividends are paid out of after-tax profits; customers usually pay
only after a profit has been earned and recognised; and capital
expenditure is for cash and only part of it quickly enters the profit
and loss account as depreciation. There are many more such
reasons and they do matter. It is quite common for young,
profitable and rapidly expanding businesses to run out of cash,
occasionally with fatal results.

*It is often said that if you look after the top line the bottom line will
look after itself. Is this right?*

We are obviously talking about the profit and loss account and no, of course it is not right. The top line (sales) is a major factor in the profit and loss account, but it is by no means the only one. Getting all the other factors (cost of sales, overheads, interest etc) right as well makes a massive contribution to a healthy bottom line. The top line is of course always important – if you are selling at below marginal cost, an increase in sales will result in an increased loss.

Many successful companies borrow a lot of money. Should we do that?

Perhaps! The position of high borrowing relative to shareholders' funds is known as being highly geared. If you do well, the returns in percentage terms will be great. If you do badly, the failure in percentage terms will also be great. So if you are confident and have reserve sources of finance, perhaps up to a point you should be highly geared, but only up to a point. It can be dangerous to go too far. Please also remember that for a very long time Lord Weinstock ran GEC very successfully with a so-called cash mountain and no borrowings at all. He was heavily criticised at the time for being unadventurous, but look at the disaster when the policy was changed after his retirement.

One of our customers has gone into administration. Does it mean that we have got a bad debt?

It might mean that, but hopefully it will not. When a company is in administration it is run by a licensed insolvency practitioner and it enjoys a period of protection from its creditors. The aim of administration is to save the company or, if this is not possible, to get the best possible result for the creditors. The administration might succeed, in which case you will get paid, though you will probably have to wait for the money. On the other hand, it may fail, in which case you will get part payment or nothing.

Our company's balance sheet has a very large sum for fixed assets, yet it is short of working capital. How can this be?

Working capital is the difference between current assets and current liabilities. Fixed assets are not part of current assets because they are not available to be turned into cash quickly. Perhaps the large amount for fixed assets is the reason for the shortage of working capital.

Our directors have ordered ten per cent across the board budget cuts. Why don't they realise the damage that they will cause?

I fully agree with your indignation. Things that should not be cut will be cut alongside things that should be cut, and possibly some things will not be cut enough. Inefficiency will inevitably follow and all the managers will have an incentive to inflate their future budget submissions. Why do the directors do it? Perhaps they are mad or perhaps they do not know better. Just possibly the position is so desperate that cuts must be implemented without there being time for the details to be considered. So perhaps they should be pitied as well as condemned. Ronald Reagan made across the board budget cuts when he became governor of California, but he soon had the sense to recognise his mistake and change his approach.

Our auditor seems to spend a long time talking to me and not very long checking the figures. Why is this?

Auditors point out that even working very hard it is usually only possible to check a small sample of the figures and entries. The increasing trend is to audit the systems, question the managers and make spot checks. I believe that the trend has gone too far, but my view seems to be a minority one.

I believe that the directors are smoothing the results to show a trend of steadily increasing profits. Can they do this?

This has been done since accounts were first produced and it still happens, though there is less scope than in former years. This is because accounting standards have become more extensive and more prescriptive and laws have been tightened, and also because, since scandals such as Enron, auditors and others have become less tolerant of the practice. One way that the figures can possibly be 'massaged' is to take a particularly hard or particularly soft view of the bad debt reserve. It does not affect the overall profit or loss in the long term, but it can do so for particular years. It is perhaps more dangerous to hold back bad news than to hold back good news.

We have just bought a large amount of stock but it does not seem to have affected our profits. Why is this?

It is down to timing. Stock purchased goes into the balance sheet as a current asset. It only goes into the profit and loss account (as a cost) when it is sold. If it cannot be sold, it must be written down or written off, or perhaps sold cheaply.

I distrust some of the figures in the budget variance report sent to me. What should I do?

You should talk to the person who produced the report. They will very probably try to help and be pleased that you are taking an interest. So look at the figures together and find out if you are right or wrong. Accountants do occasionally make mistakes, so perhaps the report is not accurate. You may find that there is a timing difference and that the accountants have put something in a different period from the one that you expected. Another possibility is that 'head office' may have dumped part of some centrally incurred costs, over which you have no control, into your particular cost centre. If this has been done, please shout at them and say that I told you to do so.

Second section

Single entry bookkeeping

As Julie Andrews memorably sang in *The Sound of Music*, it is usually a good idea to start at the very beginning, but this is starting before the very beginning, because hardly any businesses use single entry bookkeeping. It is described because it will help show why the much superior double entry bookkeeping is almost exclusively used. However, a tiny organisation, such as perhaps a village football club, just might use the single entry version.

As the name suggests, single entry bookkeeping involves writing down each transaction just once. It is in fact the simple listing of money paid and received. Every time the treasurer writes a cheque, he records in a book the date, amount and payee. Every time something is paid into the bank, the details are entered elsewhere in the book. Cash paid out or received is entered in a similar way.

If the treasurer has been very careful he can prepare an accurate receipts and payments account from the records. He would, however, be wise to prove the figures as far as possible. Cash actually in the cash box should equal the cash received less the cash paid out, after allowing for the starting balance, of course. The balance on the bank statement should equal money banked less cheques written, after allowing for the opening balance and items that have not yet reached the statement. Records kept in this way have severe limitations. Among them are:

- An item written down wrongly may not be noticed as a mistake.
- Money owing to the organisation or by the organisation is not shown. The football club accounts will not show subscriptions owing by members or the amount owing to a painter for painting the clubhouse.

- Long-term assets are not shown. £1,000 spent on equipment last year is not mentioned in this year's accounts, even though the equipment still has some value.

The concept of double entry bookkeeping

Double entry bookkeeping is much superior to single entry bookkeeping and virtually all serious businesses keep their accounting records in this way. At the heart of double entry bookkeeping is the concept that every transaction involves both the giving of a benefit and the receiving of a benefit. Consequently, every transaction is written into the books twice, once as a debit and once as a credit. It follows that the bookkeeping system must always balance, which is a big benefit. Some types of mistake will cause the system to be out of balance, and as a result the bookkeeper will be alerted to a problem.

A set of double entry records enables a complete view to be taken. For example, consider a cheque for £500 that pays the telephone bill. The telephone account is debited with £500 and this appears in the profit and loss account. Also, £500 is credited to the bank account and the running total in the account is recorded in the balance sheet.

The basic rules and disciplines of double entry bookkeeping

The principles of double entry bookkeeping were written down in 1493 by a Franciscan monk called Luca Pacioli. His work has stood the test of time because his principles are still valid today. I once wrote a book on the subject of double entry bookkeeping and on the very first page made the point that the rules and disciplines were fixed and unchanging. Despite this the publisher asked me to do a revised edition to bring it right up to date and take account of the latest trends. I felt compelled to decline the request.

A manual ledger is ruled for posting on two sides. You will very probably only ever see computerised accounting records and not old-fashioned manual records. Nevertheless, please remember that a computer does exactly what the manual records do, only it does it much more quickly and efficiently. Three basic rules should be understood.

1. Debit on the left. Credit on the right.

Why this way round? The answer to this question is the same as the answer to the question 'why do we drive on the left of the road in Britain?'. A long time ago someone decided that that is the way it would be. We all have to do it the same way, so that's the way it is.

2. For every debit there must be a credit.

This is the fundamental rule of bookkeeping, and there are no exceptions. One account gives the benefit and one account receives the benefit. Let us return to the £500 cheque that pays the telephone account. After posting, the balances on the two accounts are:

Telephone account	£500 debit
Bank account	£500 credit

The entries may be numerous and complicated but the rule still applies. Scientists sometimes help themselves remember the rule by thinking of the law of physics *'for every action there is an equal and opposite reaction'*.

3. Debit receives the benefit. Credit gives the benefit.

Again, why this way round? Again, because it was decided a long time ago and that's the way it is. This may be hard to grasp and it is probably the opposite of what you would instinctively expect. After all, your bank statement is credited when money is paid into your account. But look at it from the point of view of the bank. The bank's records are a mirror image of your records, so a credit for you is a debit for the bank. It may help you to remember the rule if you keep in mind that assets are debit balances and liabilities are credit balances. So a new van is a debit, and a bank overdraft is a credit. Also, costs are debit balances and income is credit. So wages are debit, and sales are credit.

Example of double entry bookkeeping postings

Samantha Jones runs a ladies' dress shop. One day the following financial events occur:

- She banks cash takings of £460.
- She makes a credit sale of £100 to Mrs Clarke.
- She purchases dresses from London Dress Supplies for £1,000. This is on credit.
- She pays wages of £110.
- Mrs Clarke pays £80 owing from a previous sale. This is banked.

Bank account

Debit	£	Credit	£
Sales account	460	Wages account	110
Mrs Clarke account	80		

Sales account

Debit	£	Credit	£
		Bank account	460
		Mrs Clarke account	100

Mrs Clarke account

Debit	£	Credit	£
Sales account	100	Bank account	80

Stock account

Debit	£	Credit	£
London Dress Supplies account	1,000		

London Dress Supplies account

Debit	£	Credit	£
		Stock account	1,000

Wages account

Debit	£	Credit	£
Bank account	110		

The layout of accounts has been simplified because it is only the principles of posting that are being illustrated. In real life, each entry would be dated and the balance of each account would be shown. Note that the total of all the debits equals the total of all the credits, £1,750 in each case.

The different types of account

There are five different types of account and they are treated differently when the accounts are prepared. This does not affect the bookkeeping and posting may be made freely from one type of account to another. The five different types of account are:

Income accounts
These accounts relate to sales and they increase the profit. The income accounts normally have a credit balance and are eventually credited to the profit and loss account.

Expenditure accounts
These accounts are made up of expenditure that reduces profit. The expenditure accounts normally have a debit balance and are eventually debited to the profit and loss account.

Asset accounts
These accounts normally have a debit balance and are made up of assets that retain their value. Asset accounts go into the balance sheet, not the profit and loss account. Examples of asset accounts are stock, motor vehicles and the bank account (if there is not an overdraft).

Liability accounts
These accounts are the debts of the business and normally have a credit balance. Liability accounts go into the balance sheet, not the profit and loss account. Money owing to suppliers is in a liability account. A further example is a bank account with an overdraft.

Capital accounts

These accounts represent the investment in the business by the owners. If the business is a company, they are the 'net worth' of the business owned by the shareholders. The accounts normally have a credit balance and there is something very wrong if they do not. They are credit accounts because they are money owing to the shareholders by the company. If the company were to be wound up, the shareholders would receive the net worth of the company. Examples of capital accounts are share capital account and revenue reserve account.

Trial balance, profit statement and balance sheet

A trial balance is a listing of all the balances in the double entry bookkeeping system. As every balance is listed the total of the debit balances must equal the total of the credit balances and a mistake has been made if they do not do so. Computerised systems should make a failure to balance impossible, though other types of mistake can happen. A trial balance lists the balances at a stated date. It can be done at any time but if it is done as a step towards preparing a profit statement, it is necessary to do it as at the last day of the profit period.

Every balance listed goes into either the profit statement or balance sheet. In order to prepare a profit statement, it is therefore necessary to identify the income and expenditure type balances in the trial balance and use only those. Profit statement is the name often given to an internal document setting out the trading activity and results. It is sometimes called the profit and loss account and this is the title given in the more formal published accounts. A profit statement always covers a period of time. This may be a year or it may be some other period.

A balance sheet lists in summarised form all the assets and

liabilities of the business. This gives a lot of useful information. So long as the total assets are greater than the total liabilities, the difference between the two totals is the 'net worth' of the business at book value. A balance sheet gives the account balances as at a stated date. This is unlike a profit statement which covers a stated period.

Accounting adjustments

Except in a very small and simple business, it will be necessary to make adjustments to the trial balance before preparing the profit statement. In particular, adjustments are usually necessary for accruals and prepayments, depreciation and reserves and provisions. This is partly because it is usually impossible to get everything 100 per cent up to date, and partly because the profit statement is usually a matter of judgement as well as fact. The adjustments can be an opportunity to manipulate the profit statement, though this is of course dangerous and wrong. We will have a look at the three types of adjustment mentioned above.

Accruals and prepayments

Accruals are costs incurred, but which have not yet been entered into the books. There may be two possible reasons for this:

- The books have been closed off without getting all the invoices in. This is almost inevitable. A few suppliers may be months late submitting their invoices and invoices can be held out for checking or query.
- Invoices cover a period of time and the accounts are made up to a point within that time.

An example of the second point is the quarterly telephone charge. Suppose that this averages £900 per quarter, and the quarters finish at the end of January and at the end of April. The accounts for the year to 28 February will understate the telephone charge by £300 for the month of February. The solution is to accrue £300 for the undercharged telephone account. The entries are:

Telephone account	£300 debit
Accruals	£300 credit

Accruals are money owing by the business and the figure goes into the balance sheet. When the accounts are done accruals must be entered for all items such as the telephone account and realistic estimates must be made for missing invoices. All these increase the expenditure costs in the profit statement.

Prepayments are the exact opposite of accruals. They are costs which have been entered into the books, but which have not yet been incurred. There are two possible reasons for this:

- Invoices have been submitted too soon or the books have been left open for too long.
- Invoices cover a period of time ending after the final date for the profit and loss account.

An example of the second point is an insurance invoice for £1,000 dated 1 September, and covering a year in advance. Unless an adjustment is made the profit and loss account for the year to the next 28 February will understate the profit by £500.

The solution is to prepay £500 for the six months after 28 February. The entries are:

Insurance account	£500 credit
Prepayments	£500 debit

Prepayments are money owing to the business and the figure goes into the balance sheet. All these decrease the expenditure costs in the profit and loss account.

Depreciation

Fixed assets are those that have a useful and productive life longer than the period of the profit statement. Examples are factory machinery, computers, motor vehicles etc. It would obviously be wrong to charge the whole cost of these assets to the profit and loss account in the year of purchase. The profit would be understated in that year and overstated in succeeding years. The problem is overcome by charging only a proportion in each year of the expected useful life of the asset.

There are different methods of doing the calculation, but the simplest and most common is the straight-line method. For example, let us consider a piece of factory machinery costing £500,000 and with an expected useful life of five years. The profit and loss account would be charged £100,000 in each of the five years. The bookkeeping entry is:

> Depreciation account   £100,000 debit
> (in the profit and loss account)
>
> Fixed asset account   £100,000 credit
> (in the balance sheet)

This is an illustration of how profit and cash are not the same thing. It is possible to be profitable and to run out of cash, and many businesses do fall into this trap. In the above example, cash is £400,000 worse off than profit. Of course it comes to the same thing in the long term, but not in the short term.

Another commonly used system is the so-called reducing

balance method. With this a fixed percentage of the written down balance is depreciated every year. This means that the depreciation extends over a longer period and that the asset is never entirely written off. This is often realistic because even a non-functioning wreck of a motor car has a scrap value, though old computers are usually worthless. The first three years' depreciation on the plant and machinery given above as an example would be:

Year 1 20 per cent x £500,000	=	£100,000
Year 2 20 per cent x £400,000	=	£80,000
Year 3 20 per cent x £320,000	=	£64,000

Reserves and provisions

If life was absolutely straightforward, there would probably be no need for reserves and provisions. Each transaction would be written into the books and that would be the end of it, but of course there is more to it than that. It is necessary to take a view about the probability of future events, and to make corresponding reserves in the accounts. To a certain extent a profit and loss account is a matter of opinion as well as a matter of fact. This point is well understood by accountants, but is not always understood by the public.

The bad debt reserve is one of the most common reserves. If sales are £1,000,000 and if payment is received in full, the accounting entries are:

Sales   £1,000,000 Credit (in the profit and loss account)
Debtors £1,000,000 Debit (in the balance sheet)

Debtors are people who owe money to the business. If they all pay in full, the accounting entries are then:

Debtors	£1,000,000 Credit
Bank account	£1,000,000 Debit

The final result is that £1,000,000 has gone into the profit and loss account and £1,000,000 has gone into the bank. But let us suppose that not all of the customers have paid, and that at the balance sheet date £250,000 is owed to the business. £200,000 of this is owed by the government and the directors feel 100 per cent sure that it will be paid. The remaining £50,000 is split as follows:

Jones Ltd	£8,000	100 per cent bad debt
King Ltd	£40,000	50 per cent bad debt risk
Major Ltd	£2,000	20 per cent bad debt risk
	£50,000	

It will be necessary to create a bad debt reserve of £28,400 made up as follows:

Jones Ltd	£8,000
King Ltd	£20,000
Major Ltd	£400
	£28,400

The profit, and also the money owing to the business, are both reduced by £28,400. Time will tell whether the £28,400 reserve is correct, too cautious or too optimistic. If everyone pays in full, £28,400 will be credited to the profit and loss account in a later period. If the bad debts turn out to be higher than £28,400, a further sum must be written off in a later period.

This illustrates the principles well. Reserves and provisions are necessary when something has not happened yet, but may do so in the future. The chances of it happening may vary between a virtual certainty to a slight possibility. The following are some of the circumstances in which a reserve or provision may be necessary:

1. *Warranty claims* – Consider a double glazing company that gives a ten-year guarantee on all windows that it fits. The cost of repairs over a ten-year period will be incurred without charging customers, and will relate to income that has already been credited to the profit and loss account.

2. *Legal claims* – A lawsuit may be brought in the future, relating to sales that have already been credited to the profit and loss account.

3. *Settlement discount* – Customers may be given the option of deducting a certain sum or percentage in return for payment within a specified period. It will not be possible in advance to be sure how many customers will take advantage of this. Consequently, a reserve for the estimated amount must be created. It should not be forgotten that many customers may deduct the settlement discount despite failing to pay on time. I write from bitter experience.

4. *Restructuring* – A business may intend to make a lot of people redundant in the near future and believe it right to make a reserve for the cost of the redundancies.

The last point is controversial and illustrates the fact that reserves and provisions may sometimes be used to manipulate the figures in one particular year. It does not work in the long term but it may do so in the short term. The temptation is often strong. John Maynard Keynes, the great economist, once observed that 'in the long term we are all dead'. Some directors and managers may take this to heart, especially if they intend to move on before the long term arrives.

Questions to test your understanding

1. Different types of account

For each of the ten accounts mark the type of account, whether it is a profit and loss or balance sheet account, and whether it normally has a debit balance or a credit balance.

> Stock account.
> Rental income account.
> Bank overdraft account.
> Wages account.
> Share capital account.
> Revenue reserves account.
> Invoiced sales account.
> Purchase ledger creditors account (these are suppliers).
> Trade debtors account (these are customers).
> Electricity account.

2. Accruals and prepayments

A company makes up its accounts to 28 February. The bank overdraft averages £1,200,000 and the company pays ten per cent interest. Bank interest has been paid up to 14 February. There are believed to be £80,000 invoices not received when the books are closed off.

Rent is £150,000 per quarter and three months in advance was paid on 1 February.

Please calculate the accruals and prepayments at 28 February.

3. Depreciation

A company has the following balances in its books:

	Original cost	Depreciation to date
Plant and Machinery (20% p.a.)	£100,000	£90,000
Motor Vehicles (25% p.a.)	£40,000	£20,000

Using the straight-line method please calculate the depreciation charge for a full year. *Be careful, there is a trap.*

4. Reserves and provisions

A company is owed £1,000,000. It is certain that £50,000 is a bad debt and it believes that a provision of two per cent of the remainder should be made.

Please calculate the bad debt reserve.

INSTANT TIP

Your accountants will very probably be pleased to help you understand the financial information that they give you.

02

What should I know about profit statements and balance sheets?

Companies are required by law to produce annual statutory accounts, including a profit and loss account and a balance sheet. Furthermore, numerous companies and many other businesses produce regular profit statements for the benefit of the managers, often augmented by balance sheets. These are prepared using information obtained from the double entry bookkeeping records explained in the previous chapter. This chapter explains profit statements and balance sheets under the following headings:

- The concept of a profit statement.
- Example of a very simple profit statement.
- The effect of tax on profit statements.
- Profit statement for a trading company.
- Profit statement for a manufacturing company.
- What is a balance sheet?
- Where do the balance sheet figures come from?
- Example of a simple balance sheet.

- Terms used in a balance sheet.
- An example of a company profit and loss account and balance sheet.

The chapter concludes with some questions to test your understanding of profit statements and balance sheets.

The concept of a profit statement

A profit statement is a summary of all the revenue and expense items occurring in a specified period of time. A trial balance is listed, then the necessary adjustments are made and then another trial balance is listed. The term 'trial balance' and some of the adjustments were explained in Chapter 1. All the balances of a revenue or expense nature are taken from the trial balance and all the other balances in the trial balance are ignored.

The profit statement should be properly headed and the period of time that it covers should be stated. This is often a year, but it can be six months, three months, a week or any period that the managers wish. The fact that a profit statement covers a period of time makes it fundamentally different from a balance sheet, which is a summarised snapshot of the financial position at a stated date.

The term 'profit statement' implies that it is an internal document for the use of the managers. If this is the case, it can be presented in the way that the managers think most suitable, although fundamental bookkeeping and accounting rules must of course be followed. Published statutory accounts, on the other hand, must be presented in ways prescribed by law and accounting standards.

Example of a very simple profit statement

Julia Brown writes a book. Her agreement does not provide for royalties, just a fee of £5,000 payable on delivery of the manuscript to the publisher. The costs of the enterprise are small and she pays them in cash as she goes. After receipt of the £5,000, her profit statement may well look like this:

Julia Brown
Profit statement for the year to 31 August

	£	£
Income		5,000
Less costs		
Typing costs	600	
Stationery	100	
Travel	200	
Postage	30	
Telephone	40	
Miscellaneous	120	
		1,090
Net profit before tax		3,910

The profit (or loss) is the difference between money received and all the money paid out. Julia Brown may need the profit statement for her bank and for the tax authorities, and she may use the information herself. For example, if she has spent 391 hours working on the book, her time has been rewarded at the rate of £10 per hour. The trial balance is not shown but the bank account, which is an asset account in the balance sheet, would have a credit balance of £3,910. This is as simple as it gets and hopefully does not cause you any problems.

The effect of tax on profit statements

Profit statements are usually prepared for the managers and are often done without tax being deducted. However, tax is usually payable on profits, so a profit statement may be prepared to show the profit both before tax and after tax. As Benjamin Franklin wrote 'in this world nothing is certain except death and taxes'. Julia Brown's profit statement, which appeared in the previous section of this chapter, could look as follows:

Julia Brown
Profit statement for the year to 31 August

	£	£
Income		5,000
Less costs:		
Typing costs	600	
Stationery	100	
Travel	200	
Postage	30	
Telephone	40	
Miscellaneous	120	
		1,090
Net profit before tax		3,910
Less tax		900
Net profit after tax		3,010

Usually tax has to be estimated or calculated. This is because the exact figure will probably not have been agreed with the tax authorities when the profit statement is prepared. A double entry must be posted for the estimated tax charge. It is:

Debit   tax charge in the profit and loss account
Credit   taxation owing in the balance sheet

Profit statement for a trading company

A trading company (such as a shop) buys goods, then sells them, hopefully at a higher price. This poses a particular problem for the profit statement. It is tempting to say that all purchases of goods for resale should be entered as a cost and that all goods sold should be entered as income. It is true that in the long term, and provided that all the goods were ultimately sold, this would be about right. There are two big problems with this, however:

- It takes no account of lost stock, stolen stock, shrinkage etc.
- Even though it might be nearly right in the long term, it would probably be seriously wrong in the period of any one profit statement.

The first problem can be overcome with regular stock checks. Any missing stock can then be written off. Old or soiled stock can at the same time be written down to a realistic value. The second problem can be overcome by only writing off to the profit and loss account the cost of the goods actually sold. Goods purchased in the period are irrelevant for this purpose. This is done by putting in stock at the beginning of the period, adding purchases during the period and subtracting stock at the end of the period. The following is an example of a profit and loss account showing how this has been done:

Edward Smith and Son
Profit Statement for six months to 31 July

	£	£
Sales		160,000
Stock at 31 January	70,000	
Add purchases in period	100,000	
	170,000	
Less stock 31 July	90,000	
		80,000
Gross profit		80,000
Less overheads		70,000
Net profit before tax		10,000

Note that £80,000 is the cost of the goods actually sold during the period. Stock has increased during the period, which may or may not be a bad thing. If any stock is missing or has lost value, an efficient stocktake should adjust the figure accordingly.

Profit statement for a manufacturing company

You have already seen that the profit statement of a trading company must only contain the costs of the goods actually sold. The cost of goods purchased and held in stock must be excluded. For the same reason, the profit statement of a manufacturing company must only contain the manufacturing costs of the goods actually sold in the period. The manufacturing costs of goods not sold must be excluded. As with a trading company, it will probably be necessary to stocktake at the beginning and end of the period, but if controls are very good it may not always be necessary. The principles are best shown with an example:

ABC Cases Ltd
Profit statement for three months to 30 June

	£	£
Sales		600,000
Stock at 31 March	50,000	
Add purchases	200,000	
	250,000	
Less stock at 30 June	40,000	
	210,000	
Production wages	280,000	
Other production costs	90,000	
Cost of manufacturing		580,000
		20,000
Less total overheads		60,000
Net loss for year		(40,000)

This is the first time that we have encountered a loss. Note that it is shown by means of a bracketed figure. Please also note that all the production costs are grouped together and separated from the overheads. This is so that the total cost of manufacturing can be calculated.

What is a balance sheet?

The clue is in the name. A balance sheet is a listing of all the balances in the accounting system and, what is more, it must balance. The debit balances must equal the credit balances or, put another way, the assets must equal the liabilities. Of course, not every balance in the accounting system is shown individually. If this were to be done for a major company, the balance sheet would be a ridiculously long document. In practice, similar accounts are grouped together. A company may owe 674 individual suppliers, and the total owed might be £976,159. In these circumstances, just a figure of £976,159 for creditors would appear in the balance sheet.

A balance sheet gives details of the assets and liabilities of the business, and this detailed information is often very valuable to the users of accounts. It also reveals the 'net worth' of a business, though perhaps it would be more accurate to say that it does so according to sometimes controversial accounting rules. When a business is sold it is rare for the sum realised to be the same as the 'net worth' according to the balance sheet.

A profit and loss account covers a period of time, often a year. It has a beginning date and an end date, and the period of time is stated in the heading. A balance sheet is not like that: it is a freeze-frame picture of the assets and liabilities at one particular date. If it were done one day earlier or one day later, the balance sheet would probably be different. The heading of a balance sheet always incorporates the date that it is struck. A set of accounts consists of a profit and loss account and a balance sheet struck on the last day of the profit and loss period.

As with profit statements, laws and accounting standards prescribe how a published balance sheet must be presented, what it must contain and the notes that must accompany it. All this is covered in the next chapter.

Where do the balance sheet figures come from?

In Chapter 1 the five different types of account were listed. We have also seen that the accounts must be brought up to date and that the various adjustments must be posted. These include accruals and prepayments, reserves, depreciation entries etc. After this has been done a final trial balance is prepared.

The income and expenditure accounts are summarised and listed to form the profit and loss account. The remaining three types of account are summarised and listed to form the balance sheet. The three types of account are:

- Asset accounts.
- Liability accounts.
- Capital accounts.

A balance sheet must balance, which is the same as saying that the sum of all the debit balances must equal the sum of all the credit balances. It follows that one figure for the result of the profit and loss account must be added into the balance sheet. If it is a net profit, it is added to the reserves. If it a net loss, it is subtracted from the reserves. The reserves are part of the capital accounts.

Example of a simple balance sheet

It is now time to see how this translates into a real balance sheet. What follows is a very simple example of an unincorporated sole trader and immediately afterwards are some explanations of what it all means.

Peter Grade's business is solvent, and the balance sheet does not contain anything that should cause concern. The following points should be noted:

- The balance sheet is properly headed and dated. The business is not a company, and the balance sheet does not have to conform to laws concerning published company accounts.
- The balance sheet accompanies a profit and loss account for the year leading up to the balance sheet date. This can be deduced from the section at the bottom.

Peter Grade Trading as Caledonian Decorators
Balance sheet at 30 September

	£	£
Fixed assets		
Van	4,000	
Equipment	3,000	
		7,000
Current assets		
Debtors	3,600	
Bank account	300	
	3,900	
Less current liabilities		
Creditors	400	
Net current assets		3,500
		10,500
Capital employed		
Capital at beginning of year		4,700
Add profit for year		5,800
		£10,500

- The van and the equipment are fixed assets having a long-term value. The figures in the balance sheet should be after depreciation, and this should be explained in a note.
- 'Debtors' is money owing to the business at 30 September. It is probably owing by customers, but it could be money owing by others.
- 'Creditors' is money owing by the business at 30 September.
- There is not an overdraft, and Peter Grade has money in the bank.
- There are no long-term commitments such as a bank loan or HP agreement.

- 'Net current assets' is a healthy figure, and large relative to the size of the business. This is funds available in the short term.
- Peter Grade's business has a book value of £10,500. This is what it is 'worth' according to the records. If he stopped trading, realised his assets and paid his debts, he would have £10,500. In practice, it would probably not be worth exactly this sum. Apart from anything else, he would probably hope to sell the business and get something for the goodwill.
- Peter Grade has made £5,800 profit in the year. As he is self-employed, he will probably not have paid himself a salary. If he has taken money out of the business (which is likely), the section at the bottom might well have been something like the following:

Capital at beginning of year	4,700
Add Profit for year	15,800
	20,500
Less Drawings in year	10,000
	£10,500

Terms used in a balance sheet

An explanation of the main terms used in balance sheets follows. Where these terms appear in Peter Grade's balance sheet listed in the previous section, the corresponding figure is given.

Fixed assets

These assets are a capital investment. They will retain at least some of their value over the long term and will be available to generate revenue in the long term. The long term is usually taken to be a period longer than one year. It is not right to write them off to the profit and loss account immediately. Instead, depreciation entries write them off over an appropriate period of time. Examples of fixed assets are freehold property, leasehold property, computers, fixtures and fittings, motor vehicles and plant and machinery.

The figure in Peter Grade's balance sheet is £7,000. This will be the total amount paid for the van and the equipment, less depreciation written off to the profit and loss account in the years since the different items were purchased.

Current assets

These are not assets held with the intention of generating revenue over a long period. They are assets intended for use in a short period, usually taken to be less than a year. This includes assets such as stock which will be sold. It also includes cash, bank accounts in credit, short-term investments and money owing from customers (trade debtors).

As a decorator, Peter Grade does not have stock, but he does have money owing to him and he does have money in the bank. His figure for current assets is £3,900.

Current liabilities	These are liabilities which must be discharged in the short term. Examples are bank borrowing repayable on demand, current taxation and money owing to suppliers (trade creditors).
	Peter Grade owes £400 to creditors and this is the only liability.
Net current assets	This is the difference between current assets and current liabilities. It is an important figure and is an important indicator of the ability of a business to pay its debts as they become due. If (very unusually) current liabilities are greater than current assets, the figure is 'net current liabilities'.
	In Peter Grade's case net current assets are £3,500.
Long-term liabilities	These are liabilities due for payment after more than a year. A long-term bank loan is an example.
Capital and reserves	This is the 'net worth' of the business and is the bottom part of the balance sheet. The total figure for capital and reserves is the balance sheet total. The top part of the balance sheet is 'net assets' and comes to the same total.

Capital and reserves represent the investment of the owners in the business. In the case of a company, capital and reserves may be made up of some combination of the following:

- Share capital: there may be more than one class of share.
- Revenue reserves: these are accumulated net profits from the past, after taxation, dividends and distributions.
- Capital reserves: these are reserves created in defined ways and only available for distribution in defined ways.
- Profit and loss account: this is part of revenue reserves.

An example of a company profit and loss account and balance sheet

It is now time to show how a company profit and loss account and a balance sheet are produced from a trial balance. The following is the trial balance of Caledonian Services Ltd as at 30 September. All the necessary adjustments have been made except for taxation, which will be 20 per cent of the profit for the year. Shown are the trial balance, the profit and loss account and the balance sheet. The accounts are not in a form suitable for publication.

Caledonian Services Ltd
Trial balance at 30 September

Debit balances	£	Credit balances	£
All overhead accounts	530,000	Fees invoiced – UK	600,000
Motor vehicles	62,000	Fees invoiced – Export	170,000
Freehold premises	389,000	Bank overdraft	68,000
Computer equipment	66,000	Trade creditors	101,000
Trade debtors	290,000	Taxation	13,000
Other debtors	24,000	Long-term loan	50,000
		Share capital	100,000
		Revenue reserves	259,000
	£1,361,000		**£1,361,000**

Caledonian Services Ltd
Profit and loss account for the year to 30 September

	£
Fees invoiced – UK	600,000
Fees invoiced – Export	170,000
Total fees invoiced	770,000
Less all overheads	530,000
Profit before tax	240,000
Less taxation charge for the year	48,000
Net profit after tax	192,000

Caledonian Services Ltd
Balance sheet as at 30 September

	£	£
Fixed assets		
Freehold premises	389,000	
Computer equipment	66,000	
Motor vehicles	62,000	
		517,000
Current assets		
Trade debtors	290,000	
Other debtors	24,000	
	314,000	
Less current liabilities		
Bank overdraft	68,000	
Trade creditors	101,000	
Taxation	61,000	
	230,000	
Net current assets		84,000
Long-term loan		(50,000)
		551,000
Capital employed		
Share capital		100,000
Revenue reserves	259,000	
Add profit for year after tax	192,000	
		451,000
		551,000

The following points relating to the balance sheet should be understood:

- The treatment of tax is as previously explained. The tax charge for the year is deducted from the profit and added to the current liabilities in the balance sheet.
- A bank overdraft is normally repayable on demand. A long-term loan is not repayable quickly, unless covenants have been breached. This makes it safer for the company and is why it is not included in current liabilities.
- The long-term loan is a liability and has a credit balance in the trial balance. This is why the figure is in brackets and deducted from the assets.
- The revenue reserves figure of £259,000 is as at the previous balance sheet date. The revenue reserves figure carried forward to the next balance sheet is £451,000.
- Shareholders funds are £551,000, which is the same as the 'net worth' of the company at book value. If there are 100,000 shares in issue, each one is backed by net assets of £5.51.

Questions to test your understanding

1. A simple profit statement

Henry Smith started a business as a self-employed sales agent on 1 May. Please prepare a profit statement for his first three months trading. Please ignore tax. At 31 July his trial balance is as follows:

	Debit £	Credit £
Advertising	1,800	
Bank account		18,100
Bank charges	50	
Commission received – northern region		4,300
Commission received – southern region		4,200
Computer	6,000	
Interest	230	
Leaflets	390	
Miscellaneous expenses	710	
Motor vehicle	12,220	
Office costs	1,170	
Other motor expenses	690	
Petrol	1,720	
Postage	440	
Property costs	850	
Telephone	330	
	26,600	26,600

2. Profit statement for a trading company

The trial balance at 31 December for ABC Trading includes the following:

	Debit £	Credit £
Sales		300,000
Purchases of goods for resale	220,000	
Stock (at 30 June)	120,000	
Total overheads	31,600	

A stocktake at 31 December results in a stock valuation of £90,200.

Please prepare a profit statement for the six months to 31 December. Please assume that tax payable is 25 per cent of the net profit.

3. A balance sheet

Please prepare a balance sheet from the trial balance given below. The accounts are given in alphabetical order, not in the order in which they appear in the balance sheet.

Laslo Tamasi
Trial balance at 30 April

	Debit £	Credit £
Bank account	10,000	
Capital reserve		70,000
Depreciation on motor vehicle		30,000
Depreciation on plant and machinery		140,000
Leasehold property	100,000	
Motor vehicles	60,000	
Plant and machinery	280,000	
Revenue reserves		240,000
Stock	150,000	
Taxation		80,000
Trade creditors		200,000
Trade debtors	160,000	
	760,000	760,000

Taxation is money owing to HM Revenue and Customs by the business. Depreciation must be netted off against the relevant asset accounts. This means that the difference between the two figures is shown in the balance sheet.

INSTANT TIP

Every account in the bookkeeping system must be correctly classified. One error will cause two mistakes in the accounts.

What should I look for in published accounts?

Important point about this chapter

This chapter relates to accounts published in the UK. The laws are different in other countries.

The aim of this chapter is to summarise the information disclosed in a published set of reports and accounts, and to give hints on what to look for and the significance of what you will see. It will probably be considered the most detailed chapter in the book, so we should both look at it as something of a challenge.

To get the best out of this chapter, it is a good idea to have a set of reports and accounts to hand. You will then be able to check the various points in them. It is an even better idea to have the reports and accounts for a company that you know well, and your employer is an obvious example of such a company. The accounts of any registered company can be obtained from Companies House and the first section of this chapter explains how this can be done.

Two cautions may be necessary. First, published accounts are by definition out of date. Secondly, do not neglect the notes. Remember the saying: 'The large print giveth and the small print taketh away.'

The topics studied in this chapter are:

- The obligation to publish accounts.
- Accounting standards.
- Profit and loss account and notes.
- Balance sheet and notes.
- Cash flow statement.
- Directors' report.
- Business review.
- Directors' remuneration report.
- The audit report.
- Group accounts.

The chapter concludes with some questions to test your understanding of published accounts.

The obligation to publish accounts

The directors of all companies, including even dormant companies, are required by law to prepare statutory reports and accounts, and in all cases they are required to send them to the members. In the great majority of companies, the terms 'member' and 'shareholder' are virtually interchangeable. In the case of public companies the directors must lay the accounts at a shareholders' meeting, usually the annual general meeting. The same applies in private companies, but the members of private companies may unanimously decide that they do not want this done. They must still be sent the accounts though. When the relevant part of the Companies Act 2006 has taken effect, private companies will not routinely lay the accounts at a meeting.

Having a company is a privilege and having a limited liability company is a very considerable privilege. In return for this privilege, it is a requirement that the reports and accounts be made available to the company's suppliers, bank and creditors and to the public in general. Directors do this by sending the accounts to Companies House where, for a modest charge, anyone can see them and obtain copies. Companies incorporated in England and Wales file at Companies House in Cardiff. Companies incorporated in Scotland file at Companies House in Edinburgh. The contact details are:

Companies House	Companies House
Crown Way	37 Castle Terrace
Maindy	Edinburgh
Cardiff	EH21 2ED
CF14 3UZ	
Tel: 0870 333 3636	Tel: 0870 333 3636
www.companieshouse.gov.uk	www.companieshouse.gov.uk

Copies may be obtained by using the website, telephone, post or personal visit. There is also a Companies House office at 21 Bloomsbury Street, London WC1B 3XD. The telephone and website details are the same as for the other two offices.

When the relevant part of the Companies Act 2006 has taken effect, quoted companies will be required to publish their reports and accounts on a website. Many of them already do so.

Small and medium-sized companies may file abbreviated accounts at Companies House, though full accounts must be sent to the members. However, the full accounts may omit certain information that it is compulsory to disclose in the accounts of larger companies. Subject to several conditions, a small company is one that (counted on a group basis) has a turnover not more than £5.6 million. Subject to several conditions, a medium-sized company is one that (counted on a group basis) has a turnover not more than £22.8 million. Small companies need not send a profit and loss account or directors' report to Companies House. The balance sheet may be abbreviated. Medium-sized companies must send much more to Companies House but they need not disclose turnover, other operating income or cost of sales.

Every company has an accounting reference date and the directors must prepare accounts with reference to it, including a balance sheet dated within seven days either side of it. Counting from the accounting reference date, a public company has seven months to send the accounts to Companies House and lay them in a meeting. A private company has ten months, though they need not be laid (but must still be sent to the members) if the members have unanimously decided that they do not want this done.

At the time of writing, the Companies Act 2006 has not taken effect and the position is as described above. When it does take effect, the time limit for public companies will be cut to six months and for private companies it will be cut to nine months. The privileges of small and medium-sized companies will continue, but the law will require medium-sized companies to declare their turnover.

The accounts of all companies must be formally approved by the board and the balance sheet must be signed by any director. The directors' report too must be formally approved by the board and it must be signed by any director or the company secretary.

Accounting standards

The first accounting standards were issued in the late 1960s and they have been extensively developed ever since. They are intended to ensure that accounts are prepared according to sensible and consistently applied rules, and that the accounts of different companies are prepared in a comparable way and can therefore be compared. The list of standards is now long and comprehensive.

UK standards are issued by the Accounting Standards Board and are known as Financial Reporting Standards (abbreviated to FRS). International Accounting Standards are issued by the International Accounting Standards Board. Listed companies are required to use international standards and AIM listed companies have been required to do so for financial periods commencing on or after 1 January 2007. Other companies may use UK standards but there is a trend towards the use of international standards. A very studious person has calculated that the introduction of international accounting standards has, on average, resulted in an increase of nearly 60 per cent in the length of the reports and accounts package.

Directors have an overall responsibility to ensure that the accounts give a 'true and fair view' and this overrides all other considerations. It is not a specific legal requirement that accounts conform with applicable accounting standards. However, accounts almost always do conform with applicable accounting standards. This is partly because accounting standards are generally respected, and partly because failure to comply would generate suspicious questions and partly because it would result in a qualified audit report. Very occasionally, directors do deviate from accounting standards and give their reasons for doing so. There must be a statement in the notes to the accounts as to whether the accounts have been prepared in accordance with applicable accounting standards. Furthermore, the note must give particulars of any material departure from the standards and the reasons for the departure must be given.

Accounting standards can make a big difference. There was a furore some years ago when FRS17 took effect. This standard applied to retirement benefits and forced companies in some circumstances to recognise pension fund deficits in their accounts. This had a dramatic impact on the reported figures of some companies, British Airways plc being just one significant example. It was very controversial and is perhaps one of the reasons that many companies have been trying to withdraw from defined benefit pension schemes. Of course, FRS17 did not affect the underlying reality – only the way that the deficits were recognised and the figures reported. Despite the criticisms of its detractors this seems an excellent reason for its adoption. This standard, and its international equivalent, have received the most public attention, but other standards have also been very significant.

Profit and loss account and notes

The profit and loss account must be laid out in the way required by law and accounting standards, and it must be accompanied by notes that give certain information required by law and accounting standards. Figures for both the current period and previous period must be given. Below is the key part of a recent profit and loss account (entitled consolidated income statement) of a major British company. It has been prepared in accordance with international financial reporting standards.

Your first reaction may well be that, although the key figures are given, for a company with an annual turnover in excess of £7 billion there is not much detail. When I tell you that the company's complete reports and accounts package occupies 105 A4-sized pages, this feeling may increase. You may also wonder if 105 pages is really necessary and you will not be the only person to have had this thought. To a considerable extent we must blame (or thank) accounting standards, especially international financial reporting standards. We live in inflationary times regarding the publication of words and figures. It is interesting to note that the Bible reports the Ten Commandments in 319 words, whereas the Companies Act 2006 takes 305,397 words. Even non-Christians would probably concede that the Ten Commandments have had the greater impact on the human race.

Consolidated Income Statement

	Notes	Current year £	Previous year £
Revenue	2	7,797.7	7,490.5
Operating profit			
Before exceptional operating charges		850.1	648.7
Exceptional operating charges		–	(50.6)
	2, 3	850.1	598.1
Interest payable and similar charges	5	(134.9)	(120.9)
Interest receivable	5	30.5	27.9
Profit on ordinary activities before taxation		745.7	505.1
Analysed between:			
Before exceptional operating charges and property disposals		751.4	556.1
Loss on property disposals	3	(5.7)	(0.4)
Exceptional operating charges	3	–	(50.6)
Income tax expense	6	(225.1)	(150.1)
Profit on ordinary activities after taxation		520.6	355.0
Profit from discontinued operations	7A	2.5	231.2
Profit for the year attributable to shareholders		523.1	586.2

Of course, much more information is given in the notes. This includes a geographical and segmental split of the revenue. A further note splits the profit before interest figure of £850.1 million as follows:

	£m
Revenue	7,797.7
Cost of sales	(4,812.1)
Gross profit	2,985.6
Selling and marketing expenses	(1,625.7)
Administrative expenses	(522.7)
Other operating income	18.6
Loss on property disposals	(5.7)
Operating profit after exceptional items	850.1

It goes on to give the following further split:

	Selling and marketing expenses £m	Admini- strative expenses £m	Total £m
Employee costs (see note 10A)	844.9	228.3	1,073.2
Occupancy costs	276.2	49.2	325.4
Repairs, renewals and maintenance of property	73.0	17.2	90.2
Depreciation and amortisation	243.5	30.5	274.0
Other costs	188.1	197.5	385.6
Operating expenses before exceptional items	1,625.7	522.7	2,148.4

It is not reproduced above but the same note gives the corresponding analysis for the previous year.

You will see that the profit and loss information disclosed in the notes is building up and there is much more. Compulsory disclosure (where applicable) must include the following:

Extraordinary income and expenditure
These are separate from the ordinary activities of the company and must be separated from the ordinary activities. They are not usually encountered. A hypothetical example could be the income and expenditure of a chain of florist's shops opened and closed by a quarrying company.

Exceptional income and expenditure
These are derived from ordinary activities, but are exceptional because of their size or some other factor. The redundancy and other costs of closing a division of the company could be an example of this.

Prior year adjustments
These could be necessitated by the discovery of a fundamental error in previous accounts or by a change in accounting policy. The policy on valuing stocks is a possible example of the latter as this affects reported profits. Classifying an asset account as an income account could be an example of a fundamental error. The risks of this and similar mistakes were examined in Chapter 1.

Interest payable and receivable and similar
Interest payable must be analysed between the following categories:

- Amounts payable on bank loans and overdrafts.
- Loans of any other kind made to the company.
- Lease finance charges allocated for the year.

Gains and losses on the repurchase or early settlement of debt should be separately disclosed, as should the unwinding of any discount on provisions.

Income from listed investments

Rent receivable in connection with land

Payments for the hire of plant and machinery

Details of auditors' remuneration
This must be split as follows:

- Remuneration (inclusive of sums paid in respect of expenses).
- The aggregate of other fees paid to the auditors and their associates, with a split showing the categories of services provided.
- The nature of any benefit in kind provided to the auditors.

The amount paid to auditors for consultancy and other services can sometimes be a matter of controversy. It may be bigger than the audit fee which, big as the figure may seem, might even be considered a loss leader. Some people wonder if, in these circumstances, auditors can really be objective. Auditors of course insist that they can, not least because they have so much to lose if they are not.

Employees
The average number of persons employed by the company in the year, determined on a monthly basis, must be shown. There must be an analysis between appropriate categories, as determined by the directors, of the monthly number of employees.

The aggregate amounts of wages and salaries, social security costs and other pension costs for the period must be shown.

The basis of any foreign currency translation

Details of any transfers to and from reserves

Appropriations (including dividends)

Details must be given of:

- The aggregate amount of dividends paid and proposed.
- The amount set aside or proposed to be set aside to, or withdrawn or proposed to be withdrawn from, reserves.
- The amounts set aside for redemption of share capital or for redemption of loans.
- The aggregate of dividends for each class of share.
- The amount of any appropriation of profits in respect of non-equity shares other than dividends.

Government grants

The effect of government grants on the results for the period must be shown.

Capitalisation, depreciation, amortisation and impairment

Directors' remuneration

There are separate requirements for listed companies but the following must be given for other companies:

- Amounts paid to or receivable by directors in respect of qualifying services.
- Amounts paid to or receivable by directors in respect of long-term incentive schemes.
- Any company contributions paid to pension schemes.

The following must be disclosed if the aggregate directors' emoluments are £200,000 or higher:

- The emoluments of the highest paid director.
- The value of the company contributions paid, or treated as paid, to a money purchase pension scheme in respect of the highest paid director.
- Where the highest paid director is a member of a defined

benefit pension scheme, and has performed pensionable qualifying services in the year:

(a) the amount at the end of the year of his accrued pension; and

(b) the amount at the end of the year of his accrued lump sum.

- If the highest paid director exercised any share options in the year, then a statement of this fact.
- If the highest paid director received, or became entitled to receive, any shares under a long-term incentive scheme, then a statement of that fact.

Definitions are important and there is more detail, but the above is a working summary. For obvious reasons this section of the notes is often studied with particular interest.

Pension costs

Taxation
An analysis of tax payable must be given. There are lengthy detailed requirements.

Balance sheet and notes

Like the profit and loss account the balance sheet must be laid out in the way required by law and accounting standards, and it must be accompanied by notes that give certain information required by law and accounting standards. Comparative figures as at the start of the profit and loss period must be given. Below is the balance sheet of the major British company whose profit and loss account was featured in the previous section.

Consolidated balance sheet

	Notes	**Current year** £m	**Previous year** £m
ASSETS			
Non-current assets			
Intangible assets	13	163.5	165.4
Property, plant and equipment	14	3,575.8	3,586.2
Investment property	15	38.5	38.6
Investments in joint venture	16	9.0	8.7
Other financial assets	17	3.3	0.3
Trade and other receivables	18	242.8	211.2
Deferred income tax assets	25	35.5	24.6
		4,068.4	4,035.0
Current assets			
Inventories		374.3	338.9
Other financial assets	17	48.8	67.0
Trade and other receivables	18	210.5	213.8
Derivative financial instruments	22	76.4	–
Cash and cash equivalents	19	362.6	212.6
Assets of discontinued operation	7C	69.5	–
		1,142.1	832.3
Total assets		5,210.5	4,867.3
LIABILITIES			
Current liabilities			
Trade and other payables	20	867.8	717.9
Derivative financial instruments	22	8.0	–
Borrowings	21	1,052.8	478.8
Current tax liabilities		58.7	15.5
Provisions	24	9.2	25.2
Liabilities of discontinued operation	7C	20.5	–
		2,017.0	1,237.4

Non-current liabilities

Borrowings	21	1,133.8	1,948.5
Retirement benefit obligations	11	794.9	676.0
Other non-current liabilities	20	74.8	71.8
Derivative financial instruments	22	9.5	–
Provisions	24	19.1	19.7
Deferred income tax liabilities	25	6.1	4.7
		2,038.2	2,720.7

Total liabilities

	4,055.2	3,958.1

Net assets

	1,155.3	909.2

EQUITY

Called up share capital – equity	26, 27	420.6	414.5
Called up share capital – non-equity	27	–	65.7
Share premium account	27	162.3	106.6
Capital redemption reserve	27	2,113.8	2,102.8
Hedging reserve	27	(8.0)	–
Other reserves	27	(6,542.2)	(6,542.2)
Retained earnings	27	5,008.8	4,761.8
Total equity		1,155.3	909.2

You will no doubt notice that almost every line is cross-referenced to a note. Notes must (where applicable) include the following:

Details of share capital and debentures
This includes separate details of authorised and issued capital, details of any debentures and information about redeemable preference shares.

Details of tangible fixed assets and depreciation

Details of investments
Separate details for quoted and unquoted investments must be given. Details of aggregate market value must be given if this differs from the balance sheet value.

Details of movements in reserves and provisions

Details of indebtedness
Convertible debt should be analysed between amounts falling due:

- in one year or less, or on demand;
- between one and two years;
- between two and five years; and
- in five years or more.

In respect of debt that is due for repayment wholly or partly after five years, terms of interest and repayment should be stated. So too should details of any security given. There are further requirements.

Details of any cumulative dividends in arrears

Details of any guarantees given

Details of capital commitments and other commitments at the balance sheet date

Details of contingent liabilities at the balance sheet date

Debtors
The analysis must separate sums falling due within one year from sums falling due after one year.

Post balance sheet events

For non-adjusting post balance sheet events and the reversal of a transaction which was entered into to alter the appearance of the balance sheet it is necessary to show:

- the nature of the event;
- an estimate of the financial effect, or a statement that it is not practicable to make such an estimate;
- an explanation of the taxation implications, where necessary for a proper understanding of the financial position.

Cash flow statement

Cash is not the same as profit, a point that is sometimes overlooked. The distinction is very important and it is examined in detail in Chapter 4. For all but small companies a cash flow statement is required as part of the reports and accounts package.

The purpose of the cash flow statement, which was formerly called the source and application of funds statement, is to spotlight the increase or decrease in cash between two balance sheet dates. It gives the total for the movement and shows how an adverse movement has been financed or a positive movement applied. It also shows in detail the various factors that have contributed to the movement. An example of just one of the calculations is the following:

Trade debtors at latest balance sheet	£830,000
Trade debtors at previous balance sheet	£880,000
Cash inflow	£50,000

A cash inflow has arisen because the company is owed less money at the date of the latest balance sheet. This could have been caused by a number of factors and it is not necessarily a reason for satisfaction. Perhaps the company has been more efficient at collecting its debts or perhaps it has started offering discounts for prompt payment. Perhaps trade is down and there are fewer debts to collect. Perhaps the workforce has been on strike and there have been no deliveries to customers in the month leading up to the second balance sheet date. Perhaps last year's figure was bad rather than this year's figure good.

Capital expenditure and dividends are examples of payments that take cash out of the company without having an effect, apart from depreciation in the case of capital expenditure, on profit.

Professional analysts always pay a great deal of attention to the cash flow statement, especially if they believe that the company may be short of working capital. Readers of relatively advanced years and with long memories may remember the turmoil in Britain in the 1970s. At that time there was a widespread catchphrase, sometimes attributed to Jim Slater of Slater Walker fame, that 'Cash is King'. It was certainly true that companies that controlled their cash did not fold in the way that so many others did. Another memorable phrase popular in the 1970s and subsequently is *profit is a matter of opinion whereas cash is a matter of fact*. Anyone who studied the Enron accounts would have done well to have kept it in mind.

The summary cash flow statement for the company whose profit and loss account and balance sheet was reproduced earlier is as follows:

Operating activities	**£m**
Operating profit before exceptional operating charges	850.1
Depreciation and amortisation	274.0
Share-based payments	24.7
Loss on property disposals	5.7
(Increase)/decrease in inventories	(42.2)
Increase in receivables	(4.1)
Payments to acquire leasehold properties	(38.0)
Increase/(decrease) in payables	128.0

Exceptional operating cash outflow	(14.6)
Cash inflow from continuing operations	1,183.6
Cash inflow from discontinued operations	13.9
Cash inflow from operating activities	1,197.5
Net interest paid	(129.9)
Tax paid	(101.5)
Capital expenditure and financial investment	(267.3)
Acquisitions and disposals	–
Equity dividends paid	(204.1)
Purchase of own shares	–
Other transactions with shareholders	55.8
Debt financing net of liquid resources disposed with subsidiary	–
Exchange and other movements	(2.6)
Change in net debt	547.9
Opening net debt	(2,147.7)
Reclassification under IFRS	(129.5)
Closing net debt	(1,729.3)

Directors' report

It is a legal requirement that certain information must be disclosed in the directors' report. The list includes the following but the first four of them are not required if it is a small company.

1. An indication (if applicable) of the existence of branches within the European Union

2. Details of any important events since the year end

3. The amount of recommended dividends

4. Any difference in market value of interests in land or buildings over book value at the balance sheet date

This is only if the directors believe that the members' attention should be drawn to it and in practice it is usually only done if the difference is material.

5. The names of all persons who were directors during the year
If a person was not a director for the whole of the year, the date of appointment and/or the date of resignation or removal must be given.

6. Directors' interests
This means details of each director's interest in shares or debentures at the beginning and end of the year. Interests in the shares or debentures of any other group company must also be stated. Included for each director must be the interests of spouses and children or stepchildren up to the age of 18. Any options or rights to subscribe for shares or debentures must be given.

7. Political donations
If expenditure on political purposes in the year exceeds £200, details of amounts and the name of each person or organisation receiving such amounts must be given. A wholly owned subsidiary company need not give this information, but it must be given by the holding company. The disclosure threshold will shortly be increased to £2,000.

8. Charitable donations
If expenditure on charitable purposes in the year exceeds £200, details must be given. Expenditure on charitable purposes outside of Great Britain is excluded for this purpose. A wholly owned subsidiary company need not give this information, but it must be given by the holding company.

9. Changes in share capital
This is the issue of new shares and the acquisition of its own shares.

10. Payment of suppliers

The following must be given for public companies and for large private companies that are subsidiaries of public companies:

- A statement of policy on the payment of suppliers.
- If the company subscribes to a code on payment practices, such as the CBI code, this must be stated, and it must also be stated how details of the code may be obtained.
- A statement of the average number of days' credit outstanding at the balance sheet date.

It is not unknown for companies to 'window dress' the ratio by making extensive payments just before the balance sheet date.

11. Accounting principles

Details of accounting principles adopted must be given.

12. Going concern

If applicable, directors should report:

- Any material uncertainties, of which the directors are aware, in making their assessment of the going concern status of the company, that may cast significant doubt on the company's ability to continue as a going concern.
- Where the foreseeable future considered by the directors in their assessment of the going concern status of the company is less than one year from the date of approval of the financial statements, then that fact.
- Where the financial statements are not prepared on a going concern basis, that fact, together with the basis on which the financial statements are prepared and the reasons why the company is not considered a going concern.

Business review

This is required for all but small companies and the title gives a very good indication of its purpose. It must give a fair review of the company's business and a description of the principal risks and uncertainties facing the company. This must incorporate a balanced and comprehensive analysis of the company's business during the financial year and the position of the company's business at the end of the year. More information is required in the case of a quoted company. The business review can help the reader understand the company, particularly if the directors try to be helpful rather than adopting a legalistic approach. The business review is part of the directors' report.

Directors' remuneration report

This is required for quoted companies only and, human nature being what it is, it often seems to be the most studied part of the reports and accounts package. The report must contain a mass of information about the salary, bonus, pension, share options, service contract etc. of each director by name.

There must be a separate vote on the directors' remuneration report at the meeting at which the accounts are laid. However, the vote is advisory and does not change anything, though a vote to reject the report is massively damaging and has a major persuasive effect. This actually happened in GlaxoSmithKline plc a few years ago and it almost happened in British Airways plc.

The audit report

Every company is required to have an auditor, subject to limited exceptions for small companies and dormant companies. The primary function of an auditor is to report on the statutory accounts. It should particularly be noted that they report on the accounts and express an opinion. They do not certify the accuracy of the figures. This is very widely misunderstood by the public and by some managers too.

The prime purpose of an audit report is to state whether, in the opinion of the auditor, the financial statements give a 'true and fair view'. Audit reports almost always do say this – the main reason being the skill, integrity and professionalism of directors. However, a seriously qualified audit report can be very damaging and directors therefore have a strong incentive to make any necessary changes. Some qualifications to an audit report may not be serious, such as, perhaps, a minor and technical breach of an accounting standard. The Combined Code calls for listed companies to set up an audit committee and many other companies choose to do this.

Group accounts

When two or more companies form a group the parent company is required to issue group accounts as well as accounts just for itself. These must include a group profit and loss account and a group balance sheet, and they eliminate inter-group trading and inter-group indebtedness. The balance sheet shows the group's position vis-à-vis the outside world.

To understand why this is necessary, consider three companies, A, B and C, with B and C being owned by A. A sells goods costing £600 to B for £1,000 but they have not yet been sold by B. Furthermore, A has lent £1,000 to B, B has lent £1,000 to C and C has lent £1,000 to A. Without group accounts A would declare £400 profit by effectively trading with itself and each company's balance sheet would have an extra £1,000 in both assets and liabilities.

Questions to test your understanding

1. Can anyone get hold of the accounts of any registered company?

2. Is there a legal requirement that accounts conform with applicable accounting standards?

3. Must the profit and loss account and balance sheet give the figures for the previous period and date as well as the current period and date?

4. May a balance sheet group debts due for payment now with debts due for payment in 18 months' time?

5. Must a donation of £6,000 to a political party be disclosed in the directors' report?

6. Must a loan to a political party be disclosed in the directors' report?

7. Trade debtors at latest balance
      sheet date   £706,000
      Trade debtors at previous balance
          sheet date   £671,000
      Is it a cash inflow or outflow?

INSTANT TIP

Reading the notes is an essential part of understanding published accounts.

04

Why is cash and the management of working capital important?

The effective management of cash and working capital will increase profits and reduce the risk of embarrassment or, even worse, business failure. Businesses do not stop trading because of shortage of profits, undesirable though this might be. They stop trading because they do not have enough money to pay the bills. Many profitable businesses do fail in this way, especially rapidly expanding ones. It is hard to think of more compelling reasons than these. The aspects of the subject covered are:

- What is cash and what is working capital?
- The importance of cash and the importance of working capital.
- The distinctions between cash, profit and net worth.
- The right amounts for cash and working capital.
- Connecting cash management to line management.
- The management of working capital.
- Cash flow forecast.

The chapter concludes with some questions for you to test your understanding.

What is cash and what is working capital?

It is tempting, but of course wrong, to say that cash is the notes and coins found in the petty cash box. This is part of cash, but only a very small part. Cash is the total of all the bank balances plus any notes and coins. The bank balances almost always make up virtually all the cash total. Bank overdrafts must be deducted. It is possible, and indeed very common, for total cash to be a minus figure as in the following:

		£
Bank balances in credit		1,000
Notes and coins		£500
		£1,500
Less bank overdrafts		200,000
Total cash		(198,500)

Working capital is the difference between current assets and current liabilities. Current assets are cash and assets that can be turned into cash in the short term. Current liabilities are liabilities payable in the short term. They are shown in the balance sheet and the following is an example:

	£
Current assets	
Stock	600,000
Debtors	941,000
	1,541,000

Current liabilities	
Creditors	516,000
Bank overdraft	377,000
	893,000
Working capital	648,000

Working capital is usually a positive figure and the bigger the figure, the bigger the margin of safety. If working capital is a negative figure, it is a very worrying sign of possible trouble and at the very least a reason to ask searching questions.

The importance of cash and the importance of working capital

It is possible, and indeed it is not uncommon, for a business to fail that is making profits at the time of its failure. This is because it does not have enough cash to pay its suppliers as the debts fall due for payment. Profits are obviously very desirable and very important, and in the long term they provide the means to pay the suppliers, but in the short term it is necessary to have cash.

It is possible, and quite common, for a very profitable, rapidly expanding business to run out of cash. This is because a rapidly expanding business usually has an increasing need for working capital. Cash goes out of the business before a greater amount of cash comes into the business. It may be necessary to take on more staff and pay them and it may be necessary to take larger premises. It may be necessary to buy more stock to meet the greater volume of orders.

This does not, of course, mean that a business should not be profitable and rapidly expanding. It means that the owners should ensure that it does have sufficient cash and working capital. Perhaps more share capital should be injected into the company. Perhaps steps should be taken to convert a short-term bank overdraft into a long-term bank loan. Perhaps the payment of dividends should be stopped for a while. There are many possibilities.

Working capital and cash are both very important. The control of working capital is a step towards the control of cash. If working capital is adequate, it is likely that cash will be adequate or at least that cash will become adequate in the near future.

The distinctions between cash, profit and net worth

Cash, profit and net worth are completely different things and should not be confused, though they sometimes are, especially cash and profit. Cash has already been defined. Profit is the difference between income and expenses, but not necessarily received or paid in cash. Net worth is the book value of a business as shown in a balance sheet. If the business is a company, net worth is the same as shareholders' funds. Profit and cash will be the same in the very long term but the long term may be an awfully long time arriving. The reasons for the short-term differences between cash and profit include the following:

Timing differences
Sales are usually credited to the profit and loss account when goods are delivered or services performed. Payment is usually received from customers later. Purchases are usually debited to the profit and loss account as they are made. Suppliers are usually paid later.

Fixed assets and depreciation
Cash leaves the business when fixed assets are purchased, but in the very short term there is no effect on the profit and loss account. Depreciation is a later non-cash charge to the profit and loss account.

Loans to or from the business (including bank loans)
These affect cash but not profit, though there may be an interest effect.

The purchase of investments etc
This affects cash but not profits.

Bad debt reserve etc
The creation of a reserve such as a bad debt reserve reduces profit but not cash. The later release of an over-provision increases profit but not cash.

Payment of dividends
The payment of dividends passes cash to the owners of a company. Dividends take cash out of a company and are paid out of reserves.

The right amounts for cash and working capital

It is not possible to give the 'right' figures or proportions for cash or working capital, though it is possible to state categorically that they should be sufficient. This is because businesses vary and circumstances vary. If there is a sure source of further capital or resources if needed, it may be possible to operate with smaller working capital. It is also very helpful if the suppliers value the business and are willing to be supportive.

It is possible to have too much cash and too much working capital. This is wasteful because money is tied up in working capital that could profitably be invested elsewhere. Alternatively, the surplus money could be paid out to the owners of the business. Working capital should be sufficient but not excessive. This will enable the business to pay suppliers promptly, which, as well as being fair, has many indirect benefits. One of them may be an ability to negotiate better prices. There should be a margin of safety so that the business can tolerate an unpleasant surprise, such as an unexpected bad debt. The importance of seasonal factors should be remembered. The need for working capital may vary at different times of the year.

Connecting cash management to line management

It should be normal good practice to involve line managers in drawing up the cash flow budget and in preparing periodic cash flow forecasts. They should have a lot to contribute. However, it may not be right to hold line managers responsible for the outcome. This is because much, or at least some, of the cash inflows and outflows will probably be beyond their control.

This should not stop line managers being given the figures and told that their views and contributions would be appreciated. Furthermore, line managers can be made responsible for the parts of the cash flow that they can control. For example, credit controllers, salesmen or both can be made responsible for cash receipts from customers. Bonuses for satisfactory outcomes might be considered. Buyers, the accounts payable manager or both might be made responsible for cash payments to suppliers. A treasury manager might be held accountable for the whole cash flow, or at least certain parts of it.

The management of working capital

In order to manage working capital effectively it is normally necessary to manage stock, debtors, creditors and cash. Stock and debtors are current assets. Creditors are part of current liabilities and so is cash, if there are net short-term borrowings. The four categories are examined in turn.

Stock

In a manufacturing business it is customary to divide stock into raw materials, work in progress and finished goods. Different control techniques may be applied to each category. In other types of business there will be just finished goods. It is important that stock is effectively managed and there are many factors that must be considered, not all of them financial. It is normal to try to keep stocks low and the following are some of the main advantages:

- It releases cash. This is usually the main reason.
- There may be a reduction in storage and handling costs.
- It may reduce the risk of stock losing value due to deterioration or obsolescence.
- It may reduce the risk and consequences of theft. This may have a favourable impact on insurance premiums.

All this is obviously very desirable, especially the release of cash. 'Just in time' techniques pioneered by the Japanese, especially in the car industry, are well-known methods of keeping stocks low. The rest of the world has been catching up and British supermarkets are just one example of companies that do it very well, sometimes to the displeasure of their suppliers. On the other hand, there may be dangers that should not be overlooked. These include:

- It may be possible to get keener prices if orders are individually large.
- The business may have fewer difficulties fulfilling orders from its customers.

● Just in time techniques put extra costs on to the suppliers. This is fine if they will accept the burden, but they might not or they might want higher prices to compensate.

The arguments for low stocks are usually more compelling than the arguments for high stocks, but each business should be considered separately on its merits. Stock policy should be considered and planned, rather than outcomes just being allowed to happen.

Before leaving the subject of stock, four further ways of controlling stock should be mentioned. Not all of them will be relevant to you and perhaps none of them will be relevant to you, but they are worth considering.

1. Greater efforts could be made to speed up the manufacturing process. This, if successful, would turn raw materials and components into finished goods more quickly.

2. It may be possible to get customers to make stage payments during manufacture. This is most relevant to large projects with a long period of manufacture, aircraft being a good example. Of course, this will not be attractive to the customers but it is something that can be raised during the bargaining process.

3. It may be possible to avoid holding stocks of specialised finished goods. Furniture retailers, for example, often display furniture but take orders to be passed on to their suppliers. Customers place orders expecting delivery to be in eight weeks' time or some such period. Cynics might observe that their expectations are not always realised.

4. Very sophisticated computerised ordering systems could be introduced. This may go hand in hand with just in time techniques.

Debtors

As with stock it is important that debtors are effectively managed and there are many factors that must be considered, again not all of them financial. A benefit of the effective control of debtors should be a reduction in bad debts. This is additional to the main benefit of a reduction in the need for working capital. In every case policies should be set objectively and not just allowed to happen. The most suitable policies will vary from business to business but the following are among the points that should be considered:

- There should be definite policies concerning payment periods. Customers should know them and accept them and they should be legally binding. There are obvious advantages in making the payment period as short as possible.
- Managers should check that customers pay according to the agreed terms. If they do not, they should be reminded and increasing pressure should be exerted.
- If payment is still not received, sanctions should be imposed. This usually means that further supplies are stopped and that legal action is threatened, and if necessary taken.
- Credit status checks should sometimes be made before a new account is opened.
- Discounts for prompt payment might be considered.

Some of this may sound obvious and it may be summed up as advice to practise effective control. A surprising number of businesses do not do this. They may feel that it will upset customers and make it harder to make sales. There may be an element of truth in this but, nevertheless, effective credit control is highly desirable. Do we really want slow-paying customers or, heaven forbid, non-paying customers? In any case the fears are usually seriously overstated. Most customers will respond reasonably to firm but fair credit management.

Before leaving the subject of debtors, factoring should be mentioned. This is a way of turning invoices into almost instant cash. Of course factoring companies aim to make a profit and usually succeed, so there are charges and interest to pay, but it can be attractive to a business that is short of working capital. Perhaps 80 per cent of trade debtors may be turned into cash and it is well worth considering. Factoring is explained in detail in the final chapter of this book.

Creditors

Creditors are people or businesses to whom money is owed. If HM Revenue and Customs is owed money for taxes, the amount owing is included in creditors. They are the opposite of debtors and some of the points relating to debtors may apply in reverse to creditors. There are obvious advantages in a long payment period. This will not change working capital, but within the same total the overdraft will be lower and creditors will be higher. This policy could have some disadvantages. It may annoy suppliers and they may seek higher prices to compensate. A policy of paying suppliers with an extended payment period may be negotiated with them and incorporated into the conditions of purchase. On the other hand, it may just be done without the agreement of the suppliers. As you probably know, this practice is quite common in some countries and Britain is one of them. It is not fair and it may be dangerous. Quite a few managers have a moral blind spot on this point. They are outraged when their customers do it to them, but they regard it as good business practice when they do it to their suppliers.

Bank overdraft (or bank credit balance)

Managers should manage the borrowing to obtain overdraft facilities at the best possible price and on the best possible terms. Depending on circumstances, consideration should be given to seeking a switch in some borrowing from a short-term overdraft to a long-term loan. So long as the terms of such a loan are not breached, it is not repayable in the short term and there is a corresponding increase in working capital. If the business has bank deposits instead of an overdraft, it is still important to get the best possible terms and interest from the bank. In some large companies or groups these matters will be handled by a specialist treasury department.

Cash flow forecast

For all the reasons given in this chapter it is very important that future cash flow be forecast and planned. It should be done as part of the budgeting process but cash flow forecasts should also be done during the year. The preparation of a detailed cashflow forecast will yield many benefits. Calculating and writing down the figures may suggest ideas as to how they can be improved. For example, the figures for cash payments from trade debtors will be based on an estimate of the average number of days' credit that will be taken. This will pose the question of whether or not payments can be speeded up.

When the cash flow forecast is finished, it will be necessary to consider whether the results are acceptable. Even if resources are available, the results might not be satisfactory, and improvements will have to be worked out. If sufficient resources are not available, either changes must be made or extra resources arranged. Perhaps an additional bank overdraft can be negotiated. Either way a well-planned document will help managers to take action in good time.

Nastase Trading – Cash flow forecast for half year

	January	February	March	April	May	June
	£000	£000	£000	£000	£000	£000
Receipts						
Government contracts	400	–	–	200	600	350
Other	330	310	495	512	212	570
All other income	30	30	20	60	41	36
	760	340	515	772	853	956
Payments						
Suppliers and bank interest	390	402	420	340	515	576
Salaries	81	81	81	84	84	84
Tax	–	–	68	–	–	260
Capital expenditure	–	300	50	330	40	52
All other	20	20	20	20	20	20
	491	803	639	774	659	992
Excess of receipts over payments	269	(463)	(124)	(2)	194	(36)
Add opening bank balance	100	369	(94)	(218)	(220)	(26)
Closing bank balance	369	(94)	(218)	(220)	(26)	(62)

The principles are best illustrated with an example and one is given below. Do not overlook contingencies and do not overlook the possibility of a peak figure within a period. For example, Nastase Trading is forecast to need £220,000 on 30 April. This could be correct but there might nevertheless be a need for £500,000 on 15 April.

Questions to test your understanding

Please prepare the cash flow forecast for Dracula Dogfoods Ltd for the six months to 30 June. To help you a headed form without the figures is provided.

Dracula Dogfoods Ltd expects that its customers will take an average of 60 days to pay. It is owed £1,200,000 on 31 December and it invoiced a total of £700,000 in the preceding November. It expects that its invoicing in the next six months will be:

	£000
January	530
February	490
March	736
April	811
May	580
June	590

The company expects to receive a government grant of £70,000 in March and all other income is expected to be £30,000 a month.

Monthly salaries are expected to be £60,000, but in addition annual bonuses totalling £90,000 will be paid in May.

A tax bill of £134,000 is payable in June.

Capital expenditure will be £20,000 per month but an extra £40,000 will be paid in February.

The company pays interest of 1 per cent per month on its overdraft and this is debited one month in arrear. The company takes an average of 30 days to pay its suppliers. At 31 December it owes its suppliers £612,000 and it expects to receive invoices from its suppliers as follows:

	£000
January	330
February	340
March	418
April	421
May	607
June	396

All other expenditure is expected to be £40,000 per month except for June when it will instead be £20,000.

The bank overdraft at 31 December is £768,000.

INSTANT TIP

It is quite common for profitable businesses to fail because of a shortage of working capital.

Dracula Dogfoods Ltd
Cash flow forecast for half year

	January £000	February £000	March £000	April £000	May £000	June £000
Receipts						
Customers						
Government grant						
All other income						
Payments						
Salaries and bonuses						
Tax						
Capital expenditure						
Interest						
Creditors						
All other expenditure						
Excess of receipts over payments						
Add opening bank balance						
Closing bank balance						

05

How can I use accounting ratios?

A profit and loss account is a financial record of what has happened over a stated period of time, often a year. A balance sheet is a snapshot of the assets and liabilities at the termination of the profit and loss period. In the case of registered companies, and some other organisations too, the publication of these figures is required by law and so is the publication of other information in a directors' report and elsewhere. There are many sound reasons for this but, fortunately, it provides a wealth of data available for analysis and interpretation. Unpublished management accounts may be analysed in a similar way and the pool of useful figures may be extended by certain information obtained from other sources. The current share price is one example.

The intelligent use of accounting ratios is a dynamic tool and can tell you a great deal about a business. You can get behind the figures and understand their significance. If you have the figures for more than one period, you can look for trends, which may be especially important. Accounting ratios should help answer questions such as 'should I buy the shares?' and 'is the business undercapitalised?'. They can help managers run a business successfully, plan the future and make changes. The use of accounting ratios is one of the things that differentiates proactive accountants from what is unkindly termed beancounters or scorekeepers.

This chapter commences with some advice about the right approach to accounting ratios and continues by drawing your attention to some traps to avoid. It concludes with some questions for you to test your understanding. The accounting ratios featured are:

- Return on capital employed.
- Gearing.
- Dividend cover.
- Dividend yield.
- Earnings per share.
- Price earnings ratio.
- Gross profit margin.
- Profit to turnover.
- Interest cover.
- Stock turn.
- Liquidity.
- Number of days' credit granted.
- Number of days' credit taken.

The right approach to accounting ratios

Accounting ratios are very much a hands-on, practical matter. A certain amount of work is necessary and attention to detail is important. Mistakes are possible and there may be traps, some of which are explained in the next section of this chapter. Sometimes the analysis and conclusions are so obvious that they almost jump out of the page at you, but at other times they have to be unearthed with diligent and skilful work. You should try to be methodical and just a little sceptical, and you should keep the following points in mind.

Look for an explanation

There may be a good reason for an apparently bad figure. For example, a major advertising campaign at the end of a financial period may reduce profits in the short term, despite holding the promise of increased sales and profits in the next period.

Ask the question 'What am I comparing it with?'

Most of the information is much more meaningful if it is compared with something. So compare it. Useful questions to ask include:

- How does it compare with last year?
- How does it compare with the industry average?
- Is it better or worse than budget?

Be sceptical

Financial statements are prepared according to rules and assumptions. If different rules and assumptions are used, then different results will be obtained. Published financial statements may legitimately, within certain limits, use different rules and assumptions, which in most cases must be stated. There are only self-imposed restraints relating to data prepared for internal management purposes.

In some cases the correct profit is a matter of opinion and this can be true of many of the assets and liabilities. Cash, however, is almost entirely a matter of fact. It is there or it is not there. You should always approach your examination in a sceptical and enquiring state of mind.

Look for trends

It is often very useful to examine the trends because they may be much more revealing than a single figure or comparison. Fortunately, published accounts of companies must by law give corresponding figures for the previous period. A deteriorating payment performance, for example, often indicates liquidity problems, although it can also mean that selfish managers are hoarding cash at the expense of suppliers. If a company has gone from paying in 30 days to paying in 90 days, it may be more worrying than if it has consistently taken 90 days to pay.

Look at the notes and the accounting policies
You may be familiar with the saying '*the large print giveth and the small print taketh away*'. Professional analysts always spend time studying the notes to published accounts and the accounting policies. You should do the same and you should pay particular attention to any changes in accounting policies. Laws and accounting standards govern certain information that must be disclosed in the notes to published accounts of companies, and also in the directors' report.

Be open-minded
Do not have too many preconceived ideas about what you will find. Be receptive to the unexpected.

It is for you to choose the ratios that you want to use and it is for you to decide the exact definitions. For example, you might want to use profit before tax or profit after tax. Neither is right or wrong, but it will affect the results. The choice should be a conscious decision and you should understand the consequences.

Some traps to avoid

Even experienced financial analysts can make mistakes and fall into one of the many traps that may be encountered, and it is more likely that someone not financially sophisticated will do so. Below are some of the mistakes to avoid.

Not taking full account of seasonal factors
This is a common mistake. Consider a specialist greetings card

shop that commenced business on 1 May. Information from its first two six-monthly profit and loss accounts is shown below.

	6 months to 31 October	6 months to 30 April
Sales in period	£300,000	£306,000
Net profit before tax	£18,000	£18,600
Profit as a percentage of sales	6.0%	6.1%

This appears to show a steady performance with the second period being very slightly better than the first. However, this is misleading. A specialist greetings card shop would expect, because of Christmas, to make at least 25 per cent of annual sales in the month of December. Valentine's Day, Easter and Mother's Day also fall in the second period. When all of this is taken into account, the results in the second period will be seen as disappointing. Of course, an alternative explanation might be that results in the first period are particularly good.

Not making allowances for trading periods having different lengths
Consider the following:

	10 months to 31 October 2007	14months to 31 December 2008
Sales in period	£1,000,000	£1,400,000
Net profit before tax	£100,000	£140,000

Although the second period seems better, if you allow for the different lengths the results are identical, with the profit percentage being 10 per cent in each case.

Not realising that the figures have been massaged
Consider a company that usually operates with a bank overdraft. However, the managers do not pay suppliers in the last three weeks of the trading period in order to show no bank borrowings in the balance sheet. This is unfair to suppliers but a common practice. The balance sheet will of course show trade creditors being higher than usual.

Forgetting that some things can only be known by insiders
Published financial statements reveal a great deal, but there are some things that can only be known by those with inside information. Consider two companies that manufacture and sell widgets.

	Company A	Company B
Sales	£1,000,000	£1,600,000
Cost of sales	£400,000	£720,000
Gross margin	60%	55%

Company A appears to be more efficient, but the figures could be affected by the different accounting treatment of certain factory costs, such as power and property costs. Company A might treat these costs as general overheads, whereas Company B might allocate them to production costs. Overall net profit will of course be unaffected.

Not always comparing like with like
A recent set of accounts from a major British retail company disclosed the following:

Sales for year (in £ million)	8,075.7
Trade debtors at the balance sheet date (in £ million)	44.4

You can easily work out that customers take an average of two days to pay for their purchases. The calculation is:

$$\frac{44.4}{8,075.7} \times 365 = 2.0$$

You may think that this is stunningly good, and that the company must employ the world's best credit controllers. This may or may not be true, but it should not be deduced from these figures. The reason for this is that the company is in the retail sector and the great majority of sales are made for cash. Trade debtors should really be compared with just the part of sales that are made on credit.

Now consider the widget manufacturer whose accounts disclose the following:

Sales for year   £900,000
Trade debtors at the balance sheet date   £100,000

This appears to show that customers take an average of 40.6 days to pay. The calculation is:

$$\frac{100,000}{900,000} \times 365 = 40.6$$

This too is probably wrong because sales will almost certainly exclude VAT and trade debtors will probably include it. If trade debtors all include 17.5 per cent VAT, the correct calculation is:

$$\frac{85,106}{900,000} \times 365 = 34.5 \text{ days}$$

85,106 is 100,000 with the 17.5 per cent VAT removed.

Not taking note of a change in accounting policy
Consider a company that two years ago purchased a piece of machinery for £1 million and in the first year depreciated it by 20 per cent.

In the second year the company changed its policy and

depreciated the machinery by only 10 per cent. Clearly, declared net profit before tax will be £100,000 higher than if the change had not been made. Fortunately, notes to the published accounts must disclose significant changes in accounting policies and spell out the consequences.

Failing to take full account of the notes

It is sometimes said that professional analysts spend more time studying the notes to the accounts than they spend studying the actual accounts. This is wise of them because the accounts are often just the starting point. In Britain (as in nearly all other countries) the law and various accounting standards specify a great deal of information that must be disclosed in the notes to published accounts or elsewhere.

Applying percentages to small base figures

This is best illustrated with an example. Suppose that a company has a turnover of a £1 million in two successive years. The profit in the first year is £100 and the profit in the second year is £200. It would be true to say that the profit had doubled, but such a claim should be viewed in the context of the very low figures involved.

Return on capital employed

This is often abbreviated to ROCE and sometimes given the alternative name of 'Return on investment' or ROI. It is profit expressed as a percentage of the net value of the money invested in the business.

Capital employed is the balance sheet total, which in the case of a company is share capital plus reserves. This is 'shareholders funds', which is the same as assets less liabilities. Sometimes profit before tax is used and sometimes profit after tax is used. Exceptional items may be included or excluded and so may interest. Profit after interest and after tax is the most commonly used figure.

An example of ROCE is:

	Current year	Previous year
Profit after tax (in £000s)	1,604	2,113
Capital employed (in £000s)	42,446	47,969
Return on capital employed	3.8%	4.4%

Normally, the profit for the year is compared with capital employed, as shown in the balance sheet at the end of the year. However, it is better (though in practice perhaps unnecessary) to use the average capital employed throughout the year. To obtain this you will need at least the opening and closing balance sheets.

Return on capital employed is very valuable and many people consider it to be the most important of the accounting ratios.

Gearing

This ratio compares the finance provided by banks and other lenders with the finance invested by the owners. It is much used by banks who might not like to see a ratio of 1 to 1 (or some other such proportion) exceeded. It is sometimes expressed as a proportion, as in 1 to 1, and sometimes as a percentage. An example of gearing is:

Loans	£6,000,000
Shareholders' funds	£3,000,000
Gearing	2 to 1

A company is said to be lowly geared when borrowing is low in relation to shareholders' funds, and this indicates a secure, safe position. An adventurous though perhaps foolish person might say that it indicates a boring position. A consequence is that a change in profits, up or down, will have less effect on ROCE than if the company had been highly geared. On the other hand, a company is highly geared when borrowing is high in relation to shareholders' funds, and this indicates a position that is less secure and less safe. A consequence is that a change in profits, up or down, will have a big effect on ROCE. The following figures illustrate this:

	Company A	Company B
Loans (in £000s)	40,000	160,000
Shareholders' funds (in £000s)	160,000	40,000
Gearing	1 to 5	5 to 1
Profit after tax (in £000s)	16,000	4,000
Return on capital employed	10.0%	10.0%

Both companies are achieving a return on capital of 10 per cent but Company B is much more highly geared. Now look what happens if both companies increase their profits by £3 million.

	Company A	Company B
Loans (in £000s)	40,000	160,000
Shareholders' funds (in £000s)	160,000	40,000
Gearing	1 to 5	5 to 1
Profit after tax (in £000s)	19,000	7,000
Return on capital employed	11.9%	17.5%

Your reaction may be that it is better to be highly geared. This may well be true if the business is secure and highly profitable, but look what happens if profits drop by £3 million:

	Company A	Company B
Loans (in £000s)	40,000	160,000
Shareholders' funds (in £000s)	160,000	40,000
Gearing	1 to 5	5 to 1
Profit after tax (in £000s)	13,000	1,000
Return on capital employed	8.1%	2.5%

There are of course many ways of looking at the figures and it is up to you to draw sensible conclusions in individual circumstances. It is certainly true that many spectacularly successful businesses have been highly geared but it is also true that many spectacular collapses have occurred in similar circumstances.

Dividend cover

This compares the annual dividend to equity shareholders with profit after tax. It is important because it helps indicate whether or not a company has a problem paying its dividend, and whether or not the dividend may be increased, maintained or reduced in the future. Recent figures, expressed in £ millions, for a major British company were:

Profit attributable to shareholders	523.1
Dividends on equity shares	234.6
Dividend cover	2.2 times

Dividend yield

This is the dividend per share expressed as a percentage of the current share price, which of course cannot be ascertained from the published accounts. For example:

Dividend per share	5.0 pence
Current share price	88 pence
Dividend yield	5.7%

Dividend yield can usefully be compared between companies.

Earnings per share

This is the net profit after tax divided by the number of issued shares. For example:

Net profit after tax (in £000s)	148.6
Number of shares issued	2,000,000
Earnings per share	7.43 pence

Price earnings ratio

This is one of the most helpful of the investment ratios and it can be used to compare different companies in different sectors. It is often utilised to make a judgement about whether a particular company's shares are relatively cheap or relatively expensive. The higher the number, the more expensive the shares. It is often useful to do the calculation based on anticipated future earnings rather than declared historic earnings. Of course you cannot always, or indeed ever, be certain what future earnings will be.

The calculation is quoted price per share divided by earnings per share. For example:

Current share price	£10.00
Earnings per share	£1.10
Price earnings ratio	$\frac{10.00}{1.10} = 9.1$

Many would consider this to be a low ratio so perhaps the shares are worth buying, but, on the other hand, perhaps the market has information unfavourable to the company and its prospects.

Gross profit margin

In a manufacturing or trading business, gross profit (or gross loss) is the difference between sales and the costs of manufacturing or buying the products sold. In a service business it is the difference between sales and the cost of providing the service. In both cases overheads are excluded from the calculation. The following is an example:

	£000s
Sales	371.6
Less cost of sales	221.8
Gross profit	149.8
Less overheads	77.7
Net profit	72.1

The gross margin is $\dfrac{149.8}{371.6}$ = 40.3%

Gross margin is particularly important in many businesses because cost of sales is usually by far the biggest cost. Getting a few percentage points off the cost of sales will have a big effect on both gross profit and net profit.

Profit to turnover

This is one of the simplest ratios and one of the most commonly used. It is profit expressed as a percentage of turnover in the year.

Sometimes profit after tax is used and sometimes profit before tax. Some analysts prefer to deduct interest and other financing charges. The following has been extracted from the recent accounts of a major British company:

Turnover (in £000s)	7,797.7
Profit (in £000s)	745.7
Profit to turnover ratio	9.6%

Interest cover

This is an important and much-studied ratio, especially when borrowing is high relative to shareholders' funds. This is the situation known as being highly geared, which was explained earlier in this chapter. It is also particularly significant when the interest charge is high relative to profits. Obviously a company that cannot pay its interest charge has severe problems and might not be able to carry on, at least not without a fresh injection of funds.

Interest cover is profit before interest and tax divided by the interest charge. The higher the resulting number the more easily the business is managing to pay the interest charge. For example:

Interest (in £000s)	134.9
Profit (in £000s)	850.1
Interest cover	6.3 times

Stock turn

This is the number of times that total stock is used (turned over) in the course of a year. For example:

Annual turnover	£10,000,000
Annual cost of sales (60%)	£6,000,000
Stock value	£1,500,000
Stock turn	4

There is scope for misunderstanding and it is normally applied to all stock, rather than just to finished stock.

Cost of sales should be obtainable from the profit and loss account, and stock should be obtainable from the balance sheet. However, a word of caution is necessary. The balance sheet gives the stock figure at a single date and that date may not be typical of the profit and loss period, especially if the company is expanding or contracting or if the business is seasonal. A more reliable figure for stock turn might be obtained if the average of several stock figures during the period is used, though in practice this might be difficult to obtain.

It is usually reasonable to conclude that the higher the stock turn the better, and a high stock turn is an indication that a business is being efficiently run. Some years ago certain Japanese companies became famous for their 'just in time' ordering systems, and a few even managed to maintain stock levels measured in production hours, rather than days, weeks or months. The rest of the world has been catching up and British supermarkets are examples of businesses that are very efficient in this respect, though some suppliers have been known to complain that the success has been obtained at their expense.

Despite all the advantages of a high stock turn the theory should not be tested to destruction. It is not efficient to run out of stock, have to suspend production or leave customers staring at empty shelves. It may be wise to keep higher stocks of key components or the most popular items for sale. It may also be wise to keep higher stocks if the sources of supply are insecure or not responsive to an increase in demand. A company vulnerable to industrial disputes at its suppliers is an example.

Liquidity

Companies are not forced into involuntary liquidation because they are not making profits, although this is, of course, extremely unhelpful. It is, perhaps surprisingly, not uncommon for companies to go into liquidation that are trading profitably at the time. This is particularly true of companies that have expanded rapidly. The immediate cause of business failure is usually that they run out of liquid resources and cannot pay their debts as they become due. A balance sheet will reveal vital information about working capital and liquid resources, and it is possible that impending problems may be predicted.

A balance sheet should (and a published balance sheet must) separate assets capable of being turned into cash quickly from assets held for the long term. The former are called current assets. Similarly, a balance sheet should separate liabilities payable in the short term – current liabilities – from those payable in the long term. The dividing point is usually one year.

The difference between current assets and current liabilities is the working capital. This is sometimes called net current assets, or net current liabilities if the liabilities are greater. The following extract from a balance sheet illustrates this.

	£000s
Current assets	
Cash	3
Investments	161
Debtors	1,094
Stock	1,617
	2,875

Current liabilities

Trade creditors	618
Other creditors	118
Bank	100
	836

Net current assets	2,039

Another frequently used ratio is the so-called quick ratio or acid test. This is more demanding than the working capital calculation because, of the current assets, only debtors, investments, bank and cash are used, and the total of these is compared with the total of current liabilities. Only the most liquid of the current assets are brought into the calculation. Stock is excluded because it almost always takes longer to turn into cash than debtors. If stock is excluded from the above example, the resulting figure is £422,000.

Number of days' credit granted

This is the average period of credit taken by customers in paying their bills. It may be calculated as follows:

Turnover	£1,000,000
Trade debtors	£120,000
Number of days' credit	43.8 days

The calculation is $\dfrac{120,000 \times 365}{1,000,000} = 43.8$ days

The turnover figure may be obtained from the profit and loss account and the debtors figure may be obtained from the closing balance sheet. As with stock turn, two special problems should be kept in mind.

1. The turnover for a year is compared with debtors at a fixed date. If the figure for debtors is not typical of the year as a whole, the result may be misleading.

2. Turnover will very probably exclude VAT, whereas the debtors figure will very probably include VAT. At the time of writing the standard VAT rate in the UK is 17.5 per cent. If, in the above example, all the £120,000 debtors includes VAT at 17.5 per cent, the real figure for the purposes of the calculation would be £102,127 and the revised calculation would be:

$$\frac{102,127 \times 365}{1,000,000} = 37.3 \text{ days.}$$

Number of days' credit taken

This is the mirror image of number of days' credit granted and it shows the average number of days that the business takes to pay its bills. It may be calculated as follows:

Annual purchases	£1,400,000
Trade creditors	£189,000
Number of days' credit	49.2 days

The calculation is $\dfrac{189,000 \times 365}{1,400,000} = 49.2$ days

As with the number of days' credit granted, there may be a problem with VAT being included in one figure but not the other, and there may be a problem if the balance sheet figure for trade creditors is not typical. There is, however, an additional problem with this calculation. It is that a set of published accounts very probably will not disclose the figure for annual purchases. The total figure for costs will include other things, such as wages. This means that the calculation can only be done accurately if you have access to the information, perhaps because you are a manager or because for some reason the business is willing to make it available to you.

Questions to test your understanding

Below are a summarised profit and loss account and summarised balance sheet for ABC Trading Ltd, together with certain other information. You might like to answer the questions that follow this information. The answers are given at the end of the book.

Profit statement for the year to 30 April

	£000
Turnover	44,166
Cost of sales	26,928
Gross profit	17,238
Net operating expenses	12,759
Operating profit	4,479
Interest payable	1,664
Profit before tax	2,815
Tax	561
Profit after tax	2,254
Dividends	1,133
Retained profit for the year	1,121

Balance sheet as at 30 April

	£000	£000
Fixed assets		8,902
Current assets		
Stocks	3,659	
Trade debtors	9,177	
Investments	1,231	
	14,067	
Current liabilities		
Trade creditors	5,188	
Bank	6,231	
	11,419	
Net current assets		2,648
		11,550
Capital and reserves		
Called up share capital		5,900
Profit and loss account		5,650
		11,550

Other information
1. ABC Trading Ltd has issued 5,900,000 ordinary £1 shares.
2. The current share price is £5.25.
3. Annual purchases were £32,400,000.

Questions
1. What is the return on capital employed? Please base the answer on the figure for profit after tax.
2. What is the gearing?

3. What is the dividend cover?
4. What is the dividend yield?
5. What are the earnings per share?
6. What is the profit to turnover ratio? Please base the answer on the figure for profit after tax.
7. What is the interest cover?
8. What is the stock turn?
9. What figure results if the acid test is applied? This is explained in the Liquidity section of this chapter.
10. What is the number of days' credit granted? Please ignore any possible VAT complications.
11. What is the number of days' credit taken? Please ignore any VAT complications.

INSTANT TIP

Nearly all the accounting ratios will be more valuable if they are compared with something, such as the budget or last year's figures.

06

How can I make sound investment decisions?

Some investment decisions are very easy to make. Perhaps a new government safety regulation makes an item of capital expenditure compulsory, or perhaps an essential piece of machinery breaks down and just has to be replaced. In these circumstances capital expenditure is probably essential, but it will still be important that the project is properly managed and that the best choice of equipment is made. There are usually several competing options. Many other investment decisions are not nearly so clear cut and hinge on whether or not the proposed expenditure will generate sufficient future cash savings to make them worthwhile.

Of course, finance should not be the only factor taken into account. Reliability, availability and the reputation of the supplier are among many others. However, this book is about finance and this chapter examines techniques to aid the decisions. There are many and this chapter studies four of them. The topics covered are:

- Payback.
- Return on investment (ROI).

- The concept of discounted cash flow (DCF).
- Discounted cash flow using net present value (NPV) method.
- Discounted cash flow using internal rate of return (IRR) method.
- Example using the three methods.
- Cost-benefit analysis.

The chapter finishes with some questions for you to test your understanding of the different methods.

Payback

This is the simplest of the procedures which is why it is examined first. It does, however, have significant disadvantages and it is generally considered to be not as useful as the other two methods studied in this chapter. The following is an example of a payback calculation:

A new machine will cost £120,000. It will save £60,000 running expenses in the first year, £50,000 in the second year and £20,000 in each of the next five years. After seven years it will be sold for £10,000.

The payback period is 30 months, which is calculated as follows:

	Saving £	Period
Year 1	60,000	12 months
Year 2	50,000	12 months
Year 3	10,000	6 months
	120,000	30 months

Payback uses unadjusted cash as its basis. As the name suggests, it is used to calculate the period taken to pay back or recover the initial investment. The time taken for an investment to recover its cost is commonly used as a criterion for investment decisions. Managers want to know if they will get their money back in an acceptable time. Some companies have a policy that they will invest only if they will get the money back in three years or some other such period.

One of the advantages of payback is that it is very simple and easy for non-financial managers to understand. It can also be said to be an advantage that it gives crude but very useful information. However, there are two very significant disadvantages.

1. No account is taken of what happens after payback has been achieved. In the above example there will be a continuing return for four and a half years after payback. This is not reflected and the calculation would also not be affected if the machine is forecast to be scrapped with NIL value one day after the payback date.

2. No account is given to the benefit of holding money. The £10,000 saved in year three is given exactly the same weight as the first £10,000 paid out on day one. In fact inflation and loss of interest are very likely to mean that it is less valuable. The disadvantage is most significant when interest rates and inflation are high.

Return on investment (ROI)

A very useful benefit of ROI is that the answer is expressed as a percentage. Furthermore, unlike payback, relevant figures over the whole life of the asset are brought into the calculation. It is relatively simple and easy to understand, though not as simple and easy to understand as payback.

The main disadvantage is that, like payback, no account is given of the benefit of holding money. If the figures used in the payback calculation are used again, the £10,000 saved in year three is once more exactly the same weight as the first £10,000 paid out on day one. In fact, inflation and loss of interest are very likely to mean that it is less valuable. The disadvantage is most significant when interest rates and inflation are high.

There are several methods for calculating ROI and the results may differ according to the method selected. Managers are probably well advised to select the method that they think is the most appropriate and then use it consistently. The methods most used are based on average profits and average investment, and total profits and total investment. These methods are expressed in the following formulas:

$$ROI = \frac{\text{Estimated average profits} \times 100}{\text{Estimated average investment}}$$

and

$$ROI = \frac{\text{Estimated total profits} \times 100}{\text{Estimated total investment}}$$

The two ROI calculations are well illustrated by using the same assumptions that were used in the payback calculation.

A new machine will cost £120,000. It will save £60,000 running expenses in the first year, £50,000 in the second year and £20,000 in each of the next five years. After seven years it will be sold for £10,000.

Calculation of ROI using average profits method

Additional profits (before depreciation)

	£
Year 1	60,000
Year 2	50,000
Year 3	20,000
Year 4	20,000
Year 5	20,000
Year 6	20,000
Year 7	20,000
	210,000
Less depreciation	110,000
Profit after depreciation	100,000

Average profit per year is $\dfrac{100,000}{7}$ = £14,286

Average investment

	£
Initial investment	120,000
Less residual value	10,000
	110,000

Average investment is $\dfrac{110,000}{2}$ = £55,000

Return on investment is $\dfrac{14,286 \times 100}{55,000}$ = 26.0%

Calculation of ROI using total profits method

	£
Initial investment	120,000
Profit after depreciation (see above)	100,000

Return on investment is $\dfrac{100,000}{120,000}$ = 83.3%

The concept of discounted cash flow (DCF)

Discounted cash flow, like the other methods, measures the expected profitability of an investment project. In addition it takes account of the timing of cash going out and coming in. Cash paid out now is effectively more valuable than cash paid out in the future, and cash received now is effectively more valuable than cash received in the future. It is generally accepted that this makes DCF superior to payback, ROI and other methods that do not take account of the value of holding money.

DCF suffers from an inevitable extra uncertainty factor compared with payback and ROI. This is because the future value of holding or not holding money (the discount factor) must be brought into the calculation. If it is a two-year project, a value must be selected for cash flow in two years time. In benign economic conditions it might be reasonable to make certain assumptions, though economists and politicians have often got it wrong. However, if it is a seven-year project and economic conditions are volatile, the uncertainty must be considerable. Despite this, DCF is still superior to payback and ROI.

There are two main ways of applying discounted cash flow. They are net present value (NPV) and internal rate of return (IRR) and they are considered in turn below.

Discounted cash flow using net present value (NPV) method

As the words imply, future cash flow is discounted to net present value. You can choose the most suitable discount rate but one of several possibilities is the cost of borrowing. Net present day value can be obtained from published tables but it can also be calculated. For example, if a discount rate of 8 per cent is used, £1,000 received in four years' time has a net present value of £716.39. The calculation is £1,000 x 0.92 x 0.92 x 0.92 x 0.92 = £716.39.

Fairly obviously, the higher the discount rate, the less future cash receipts will be worth at net present value. The discount rate chosen can make a big difference as is shown by the following table using discount factors of 4 , 8, 10 and 15 per cent

	4%	8%	10%	15%
Year 1	0.962	0.926	0.909	0.870
Year 2	0.925	0.857	0.826	0.756
Year 3	0.889	0.794	0.751	0.658
Year 4	0.855	0.735	0.683	0.572
Year 5	0.822	0.681	0.621	0.497

Using a discount rate of 15 per cent the value of money is halved in five years. At 4 per cent it takes 17 years.
The principles are explained with two examples:

Example 1
A new machine will cost £120,000. It will save £60,000 running expenses in the first year, £50,000 in the second year and £20,000 in each of the next five years. After seven years it will be sold for £10,000. All the savings are (unrealistically) assumed to occur on the last day of the year. The business pays 9 per cent p.a. on its capital and this is the discount rate chosen.

Year 1
Discounted saving is £60,000 × 0.91 = £54,600
Year 2
Discounted saving is £50,000 × 0.91 × 0.91 = £41,405
Year 3
Discounted saving is £20,000 × 0.91 × 0.91 × 0.91 = £15,071
Year 4
Discounted saving is £20,000 × 0.91 × 0.91 × 0.91 × 0.91 = £13,715

Year 5
Discounted saving is £20,000 × 0.91 × 0.91 × 0.91 × 0.91 ×
0.91 = £12,481
Year 6
Discounted saving is £20,000 × 0.91 × 0.91 × 0.91 × 0.91 ×
0.91 × 0.91 = £11,357
Year 7
Discounted saving is £30,000 (£20,000 savings plus £10,000
sale proceeds) × 0.91 × 0.91 × 0.91 × 0.91 × 0.91 × 0.91 ×
0.91 = £15,502

Summary

	£	£
Expenditure		120,000
Year 1 discounted saving	54,600	
Year 2 discounted saving	41,405	
Year 3 discounted saving	15,071	
Year 4 discounted saving	13,715	
Year 5 discounted saving	12,481	
Year 6 discounted saving	11,357	
Year 7 discounted saving	15,502	
		164,131

Net saving discounted to net present value (44,131)

Example 2
*The purchase of two competing pieces of machinery is under
consideration. Machine A costs £100,000 and will save £60,000 in
year one and £55,000 in year two. Machine B costs £90,000 and
will save £55,000 in both year one and year two. The savings are
taken to occur at the end of each year and the company believes
that the money saved will earn 10 per cent p.a. in bank interest. A
discount factor of 10 per cent is therefore used.*

The calculations are:

	Machine A	Machine B
Expenditure now	£100,000	£90,000
Less year 1 savings (discounted)	£54,000	£49,500
	£46,000	£40,500
Less year 2 savings (discounted)	£48,600	£44,550
Savings at net present value	£2,600	£4,050

The example has of course been unrealistically simplified and, in particular, no account is taken of what happens after year two. However, it shows that after bringing the future values back to net present value the outlay is recovered in both cases, and that the result is better for Machine B. However, the result can hardly be described as exciting.

Discounted cash flow using internal rate of return (IRR) method

The IRR method identifies the discount rate that would make the net present value of the project zero. This is instead of selecting the discount rate and then seeing what the result is. It may be slightly harder to understand and it is harder to do the calculations, though computer programmes will do it for you.

If you fancy doing it manually, you will probably use trial and error to get the rate. In this case you must do the calculations based on a speculative rate, then assess the result and do it again with a different rate. After a few attempts you should fix a rate that is good enough for all practical purposes.

The answer will be expressed as a percentage in the form, for example, 'a discount rate of 13.2 per cent would give an NPV of zero'. Managers must then assess whether or not the percentage justifies proceeding with the project.

Machine A in the second example in the previous section can be used to show how it works. It is necessary to use a discount rate of 9.1 per cent to give an NPV of zero. The calculation is as follows:

Expenditure now	£100,000
Less year 1 savings (discounted)	£54,540
	£45,460
Less year 2 savings (discounted)	£45,445
Savings at net present value	(£15)

A difference of £15 is likely to be good enough for almost all practical purposes.

Example using the three methods

A new computer system and associated software will cost £250,000. It is expected that cost savings of £100,000 a year will be obtained and that the savings will be achieved evenly during each year. After three years the computer and software will be obsolete and will have NIL value. The management only wants to proceed with the purchase if a discounted return on capital investment of 12 per cent can be achieved.

In the writer's opinion managers should perhaps be suspicious of both the costs and the savings, especially if the government has any involvement. Computer projects have a nasty habit of overrunning and failing to deliver all the expected savings. You can probably think of examples.

Payback

	Saving £	Period
Year 1	100,000	12 months
Year 2	100,000	12 months
Year 3	50,000	6 months
	250,000	30 months

Return on investment (using the average profits method)
Additional profits (before depreciation)

	£
Year 1	100,000
Year 2	100,000
Year 3	100,000
	300,000
Less depreciation	250,000
Profit after depreciation	50,000

Average profit per year is $\dfrac{50,000}{3} = £16,667$

Average investment $\dfrac{250,000}{2} = £125,000$

Return on investment is $\dfrac{16,667 \times 100}{125,000} = 13.3\%$

Discounted cash flow

Year 1
Discounted saving is £100,000 × 0.94 = £94,000

Year 2
Discounted saving is £100,000 × 0.94 × 0.88 = £82,720

Year 3
Discounted saving is £100,000 × 0.94 × 0.88 × 0.88
= £72,793

Summary

	£	£
Expenditure		250,000
Year 1 discounted saving	94,000	
Year 2 discounted saving	82,720	
Year 3 discounted saving	72,793	
		249,513
		487

Conclusion
Although the ROI is more than 12 per cent, the proposed purchase of the new computer system and associated software will not quite achieve the required discounted return of 12 per cent.

Cost-benefit analysis

This is the most controversial of the methods examined in this chapter. It hinges on putting financial values on costs and benefits that are not intrinsically expressed in financial terms. These values and costs are then compared with values and costs that are intrinsically expressed in financial terms. Resulting future cash flow may be discounted to present value according to the principles of discounted cash flow.

For example, a product manager may compare manufacturing and marketing expenses to projected sales for a proposed product, and only decide to produce it if he expects the revenues to recoup the costs eventually. This is fairly straightforward and not really controversial. The costs will probably be known and the benefits will probably be estimated.

It can be much more difficult and controversial, however. Monetary values may be assigned to less tangible effects, such as risk, loss of reputation, market penetration etc. For example, the British government may consider widening a motorway by adding an extra lane. The costs of the widening should be known, though mistakes may of course be made, but how does one value the benefits? Perhaps pounds per hour can be assigned to the time that travellers are trapped in traffic congestion. Even more controversially, perhaps, a monetary value can be put on lives saved and injuries not suffered due to a reduction in accidents.

The most controversial example known to the writer is a foreign car manufacturer that made and sold a model with a design flaw. Cost-benefit analysis indicated that it was cheaper to settle the law suits than to recall the cars for modification. Stories like this make sensational reading, but of course they are most exceptional.

Perhaps the biggest problem is the practicality of assigning costs and values. Let us return to the project to widen a motorway. Should we value people's time at £10 per hour or £12 per hour? And should we value the time of business motorists more highly than the time of leisure motorists? It may make all the difference between declaring the new motorway lane viable or not viable. Of course, just because it is difficult it does not follow that it should not be done. Cost-benefit analysis can be, and often is, a valuable tool.

Questions to test your understanding

A new lorry will cost £40,000. It is expected that there will be cost savings of £12,000 per year for five years and that the lorry will then be sold for £6,000. Please calculate:

1. Payback

2. Return on investment. Please use the average profits method.

3. The saving using discounted cash flow (NPV method). Please use a discount factor of 10 per cent p.a. and assume that the savings all occur at the end of the corresponding year.

INSTANT TIP

Discounted cash flow is generally accepted as being superior to investment assessment techniques that do not take account of the benefit of holding money.

07

What should I know about budgets?

Budgets may well affect non-financial managers more than any of the other subjects covered in this book. The topics covered are:

- What are budgets and why have them?
- Different approaches to budgeting.
- Limiting factors.
- Zero-based budgets.
- Flexible budgets.
- Steps to budget preparation, approval and subsequent monitoring.
- Sales and revenue budgets.
- Revenue expenditure budget.
- Profit and loss budget.
- Capital expenditure budget.
- Cash budget.
- Budgeted balance sheet.
- Monitoring results against the budget.

The chapter concludes with some questions for you to test your understanding.

What are budgets and why have them?

The terms 'plan', 'forecast' and 'budget' are often confused and used interchangeably. This is understandable but wrong, because they are different things. It is a good start to define the terms.

Plan

This is a set of approved policies for the future and they need not be expressed in financial terms. For example, there may be a plan to achieve a position where 50 per cent of a country's population recognises a company's name.

Forecast

This is a prediction of what will happen. It differs from a budget in that it is not a target.

Budget

This is a plan expressed in financial terms. There may be a single budget or, more usually, a number of linked budgets. The key is that they are all expressed in financial terms. A budget sets targets that it is hoped and planned will be met.

Why bother with budgets? Not everyone thinks that we should and not all businesses have them. They take a great deal of management time to prepare and management time is valuable and often in short supply. Nevertheless, they do have great value which is why most businesses, including virtually all significant businesses, do have them.

Budgets enable, or perhaps force, managers to plan ahead logically and constructively. They enable, or perhaps force, top managers to see how different parts of the business interact. They enable managers to anticipate any limiting factors and plan how they can be overcome. For example, a business may be steadily expanding in a profitable and satisfactory manner, but budgeting may reveal an impending shortage of working capital or storage facilities.

Even if nothing whatsoever is done with the completed budgets, the discipline of preparing them forces managers to plan the future logically. This means considering such things as:

- Where do we intend to be at the end of the budget period?
- How a department and budget interacts with other departments and other budgets.
- Are there any limiting factors and what are they?
- What actions must be taken to achieve the budgeted results?
- What are realistic, achievable targets to set ourselves?

Of course, it is highly desirable that the budgets are afterwards used as a control tool and most organisations do this. Regular reports should enable managers to see departures from the budgeted figures and take correcting action. This is covered in detail later in this chapter.

Different approaches to budgeting

There are many different approaches to budgeting but two in particular should be mentioned.

Bottom-up method

Each manager and department is required to submit budget proposals. They are given few, if any, targets and are simply encouraged to submit good proposals in the interests of the organisation. When all the budget proposals have been received, they are collated into the master budgets, which may or may not be acceptable. If they are not acceptable, then top management calls for revisions.

Top-down method

Top management issues budget targets. Lower levels of management must then submit proposals that achieve these targets.

Each method has advantages and disadvantages. The bottom-up method may encourage managers to be innovative and realistic, and they may later feel more committed to the budgets that they have shaped. On the other hand, they may be lazy and make unrealistic submissions. When using the bottom-up method, managers will still need to be informed of limiting factors in other departments, and it may be helpful for them to be informed of significant parameters.

In practice, there is often less difference between the two methods than might be supposed. It is important that, at some stage, there is a full and frank exchange of views. Everyone should be encouraged to put forward any constructive point of view, and everyone should commit themselves to listening with an open mind. Needless to say, top management will and should have the final decisions.

Different organisations may have different policies about how challenging the budget targets should be. If the targets are too easy, they will not challenge the managers. If they are too hard, they will be unrealistic and the organisation will inevitably fail to meet them. A good compromise (and one that I recommend) is to make the budget objectives challenging but definitely achievable.

Regardless of whether the bottom-up or top-down method is adopted, it is common and sensible for top management to issue certain budget assumptions before the exercise commences. Examples might be 'five per cent wage increases from 1 July' and 'interest rates to remain unchanged'.

When the budgets are finished, the results may or may not be satisfactory. If they are not, top management must call for changes to be made. It is much better, though more difficult and time consuming, to examine each part of the budget on its merits. The alternative is to order across the board cuts. This is very demotivating for managers, especially those who have conscientiously submitted tight, realistic proposals. They are quite likely to react by, next time, submitting inflated budgets incorporating room for the anticipated mandatory cuts.

Many businesses adopt annual budgeting and often this is very sensible. Some activities are geared to an annual cycle, the Christmas trade being one possible example, and it matches obligations to provide annual statutory accounts and an annual tax return. Furthermore many businesses use 12-monthly divisions within an annual budget. This is entirely a matter of choice. Budgets are for internal use only and managers can and should select periods that suit their needs best. They must all do the same thing, however. Perhaps 13 four-weekly periods should be adopted.

Limiting factors

It frequently happens that limiting factors will be encountered when preparing a budget. These are things that stop activity beyond a certain point. Possible examples are:

Internal factors
- Shortage of working capital.
- Factory capacity.
- Shortage of trained staff.

External factors
- Market saturation.
- Availability of components.
- Activity of competitors.

When a limiting factor is encountered it is necessary to choose between two options:

1. Accept the limiting factor and limit activity accordingly.

2. Take action to overcome the limiting factor. For example, if a shortage of working capital is the problem, plans may be made to issue new shares or increase borrowing. If the problem is a shortage of trained staff, a recruitment and training programme may be planned.

Some limiting factors may be relatively easy to overcome, whereas others may be difficult or even impossible. The existence of a limiting factor is likely to have a knock-on effect over several different budgets. For example, if shortage of working space is a limiting factor and purchasing bigger premises is the solution, there will be a knock-on effect for the cash budget and balance sheet. It may well be that dealing with a limiting factor will expose another limiting factor somewhere else.

The likely existence of limiting factors means that it is important that different parts of an organisation talk to each other when budgeting. What each one does will affect others. It also means that the budgets cannot be finalised until the profit and loss, cash and balance sheet budgets have been agreed.

Zero-based budgets

The philosophy of zero-based budgeting is that every part of the budget must be formulated on its merits and without reference to what has happened in the past. This differs from the more usual baseline budgeting, where the budget may largely be based on adapting what has previously happened.

It is worth illustrating this with a very simple example. Let us suppose that last year's wage bill was £1 million. Baseline budgeting might take last year's figure plus a wage rise of 5 per cent giving a total of £1,050,000. Zero-based budgeting, on the other hand, would mean that the justification for each employee must be examined and the anticipated wages of each employee must be examined. This might give a result of £1,050,000, but it might give a very different figure.

Zero-based budgeting has definite advantages. It should help identify and eliminate waste. It encourages managers to find cost-effective ways to improve operations and it may motivate them towards being innovative and more efficient. It should also encourage the efficient allocation of resources and detect inflated budgets.

Despite all this, there are major disadvantages to zero-based methods. The most obvious is the amount of time and complexity involved in the process. Without the benefit of historical or budgeted data on which to base their assumptions, managers may unnecessarily be forced to justify routine operations. Some businesses have predictable operations that vary little over time. It is neither efficient nor effective for a manager to spend a great deal of effort developing data that could be obtained quickly and accurately by extrapolating historical data.

Flexible budgets

Consider the following:

	Budget	**Actual**
Units sold	10,000	6,349
Units produced	10,100	6,567
Factory wages	£1,000,000	£936,117

At first glance, factory wages are £63,883 below budget, which is cause for satisfaction. However, a second and more thoughtful examination will reveal that sales and production are both massively under budget. After taking this into account, it is probably correct to conclude that factory wages were, in fact, very unsatisfactory. This illustrates an advantage of flexible budgets. In such budgets, related costs are budgeted at different levels to accommodate a range of possible outcomes. Meaningful budgets are then available to compare with actual figures, even though events may not turn out as predicted.

A flexible budget may be defined in one of two ways:

1. A budget which allows for variations in cost for each selected level of output over a range of possible outputs.

2. A budget which is added to and adjusted each quarter (or other period) so that there is no artificial break-off period. The cumulative results and their effect on future planning can be seen quite readily.

Flexible budgets are also known as rolling budgets and moving annual total budgets.

Steps to budget preparation, approval and subsequent monitoring

There is a range of successful budget routines, but the following plan may be suitable for many businesses. It encompasses a set of interlocking budgets and may perhaps be right for a large company. It is in any case worth considering.

1. Top management issues the budget forms and the budget timetable. If it is following the 'top down' philosophy this will be accompanied by a note of key targets that must be achieved. If top management has authoritarian inclinations but does not wish to go quite this far, it may instead issue guidelines, parameters and exhortations. In any case, it is often helpful for top management to provide assumptions that should be incorporated into the budget. These may cover such things as anticipated actions of competitors and company pricing policy. The budget forms may be for just the summarised results or they may go into more detail. They may, for example, include a form for each category of expenditure within a cost centre, showing calculation details as well as month-by-month totals.

2. The budgets critical to the other budgets are prepared. These usually include the sales budget. They are reviewed by top management and changes are made if necessary.

3. The other budgets that contribute to the overall profit budget are prepared and submitted. This includes the capital expenditure budget because of its effect on the

depreciation charge. They are reviewed by top management and the overall profit budget is prepared. Changes are made as appropriate and all budgets of a revenue and profit nature are provisionally agreed.

4. The cash budget and the forward balance sheet are prepared.

5. Assuming that everything is satisfactory, or at least acceptable, all the budgets are formally agreed by top management. Managers are informed and they are given copies of the approved budgets for which they are responsible. In a big organisation it is normal to do this in a pyramid structure. Directors will have all the budgets but junior managers might have just the expenditure budget for a particular cost centre.

6. Managers are expected to work to the budgets and are given regular budget variance reports showing progress.

These budget routines may be criticised on the grounds that they are rather rigid and formal. For this reason managers may find it hard to feel committed to the budgeting process and the resulting budgets. It is probably a good idea to try and involve managers more than the above rules would indicate, and this could well include a greater flow of information to them. It is certainly important that people talk to each other and do not lock themselves into their own budgetary boxes.

Budgeting will inevitably throw up a number of 'chicken and egg' dilemmas. You cannot finalise A until you know B, but, on the other hand, you cannot fix B until A has been decided. For example, you cannot fix the charge for bank interest in the revenue budget until you have finished the cash budget, but this budget cannot be finalised until the revenue budget has been completed. Computer modelling will help, or you could resort to repeated adjustments until you get it right.

Computers have made it easier and quicker to prepare budgets and change them. A change to a budget has knock-on effects elsewhere in the budget and in others too. In the past this often involved much manual recalculation and muttering, with the result that changes were usually kept to a minimum. Now it is easy, perhaps all too easy. If the necessary relationships have been set up, a change will automatically cascade through the budgets. This is one of the many ways that computers save time for managers. So just why do so many of them, in Britain at least, get home from work later than their parents and grandparents did? It is a great mystery.

Sales and revenue budgets

The title of this section implies that, although they are closely linked, there are two separate budgets. This is usually the case because there is normally a period of time between taking an order and raising an invoice, and a further delay in receiving payment. It may therefore be that an order taken in January is fulfilled in April, with the cash budget not being affected until payment is received in June. This is, of course, not always the case and a retail shop selling for cash is an obvious exception.

The sales budget is a key budget because so much else depends on it. A company that has no sales has no business, and a company that only has small sales has only a small business. The rest of the company must budget to support the level of sales that will be achieved, with production and perhaps overheads expanding if the sales budget indicates increased activity.

Budgeting sales is harder than budgeting costs. This is because costs to a large extent are, or at least should be, within the control of managers. Sales, on the other hand, are only partly within the control of managers. They are also within the control of the customers, and customers will be influenced by the activity of competitors. The sales budget should be based on a number of assumptions, either fixed by the sales managers or given to them. These will cover such things as advertising and marketing support and, critically, pricing policies.

It is desirable that the sales budget be broken down to give details of unit sales, products and regions as appropriate. If the business sells overseas it is probably beneficial to separate export sales from the home market. There are two reasons for this, the first being that working with these details is likely to result in a better budget. The second reason is that it will later be useful to compare the detailed actual results with detailed budget figures. A section of the sales budget might look like the following.

Northern region sales budget

	January £	February £	March £
Product A	16,000	12,000	17,000
Product B	13,000	13,000	13,000
Product C	40,000	45,000	50,000
	69,000	70,000	80,000

After the sales budget has been agreed, the revenue budget can be agreed. This is the income part of the profit and loss budget and it should be invoiced sales rather than cash receipts. Assuming that it takes an average of 30 days to turn orders into invoiced sales and that December orders in the northern region totalled £47,000, the above sales budget might slot into a company's revenue budget as follows.

Revenue budget

	January £	February £	March £
Northern region	47,000	69,000	70,000
Southern region	51,000	58,000	78,000
Total invoiced sales	98,000	127,000	148,000

Revenue expenditure budget

Revenue expenditure is all the expenditure that goes into the profit and loss account and thus reduces the profit. This will be nearly all the expenditure. However, capital expenditure will be excluded, though depreciation is revenue expenditure.

If the business is a manufacturing business, it is normal to have a separate budget for the cost of manufacturing. If the business is a trading business, such as a wholesaler or retailer, it is usual to put the costs of the products sold into the profit and loss budget under the heading 'cost of sales'.

The revenue expenditure budget will be divided into cost centres for sections or departments. Examples are the sales and finance departments, and there will usually be one manager responsible for each department and all the costs within it. Within each department there will be a number of cost categories and there should be detailed budget calculations for each one. For example, the cost categories within the sales department will include salaries, travel, hotels, meals, entertaining, stationery etc.

Non-financial managers are perhaps more likely to be involved with the revenue expenditure budget than with any of the other budgets. This is because they may be responsible for the costs of running a particular department.

Profit and loss budget

This brings together all the budgets of a profit and loss nature into a single document. It will, of course, reveal the total budgeted profit (or loss) for the year, and for this reason it is likely to be considered the most important of the budgets. This is understandable and probably correct, but the importance of the other budgets should not be overlooked.

Capital expenditure budget

It should be remembered that capital expenditure is the purchase of items that will have a value to the business in the long term, which is usually taken to mean more than one year. This is as opposed to revenue expenditure, which is short term. Capital expenditure is divided into categories such as freehold property, leasehold property, plant and machinery, fixtures and fittings, computers and motor vehicles.

The capital expenditure budget is vastly important in some companies and the big oil companies come to mind as an example. In their case this particular budget will be counted in billions. It is much less important in many other companies and may be virtually non-existent in small service companies, though any company cars should not be overlooked.

The capital expenditure budget has significant knock-on effects into other budgets. Capital expenditure goes into the balance sheet as part of fixed assets, then it is released into the revenue expenditure budget over a number of years as depreciation. The purchase of fixed assets affects the cash budget and thus it indirectly affects the interest charge in the revenue expenditure budget.

It is important to get the timing right. Expenditure on a big project may be over a number of months or an even longer period. Cash will be affected as money is spent but depreciation usually only starts when the project is completed. If plant and machinery is depreciated over four years, a new machine costing £400,000 will result in a charge of £100,000 to the revenue expenditure budget if it is budgeted for day one of the annual budget. If, on the other hand, it is budgeted for the first day of the tenth month, the depreciation charge will be only £25,000.

If the figures in the capital expenditure budget are really significant, it may be desirable to budget for known items individually, then add a small contingency for each month.

Managers should be prepared, and perhaps required, to justify in detail their budget proposals. The techniques explained in Chapter 6 may be very relevant. If proposed capital expenditure is high, and especially if cash is tight, the capital expenditure budget is likely to be scrutinised very carefully by top management. This is because it may be a place where big cuts may be made. Perhaps the expenditure is not really essential or perhaps it can wait a bit longer. Must company cars really be replaced this year? I once worked for a company where capital expenditure was high and cash was always tight. To the annoyance of the managers, a very expensive item of capital expenditure had been cut from the budget in six successive years, even though it was justified by investment criteria. When I left, it was in the budget for the seventh time and it looked as though it would at last survive the cuts.

Cash budget

The cash budget is usually one of the last to be prepared. This is for the very good reason that nearly all its figures come from the other budgets and it cannot properly be done until these have been completed. There are many similarities with a cash flow forecast which was explained in Chapter 4 and it may be worth having another look at this chapter.

Appropriate figures are taken from the other budgets and slotted into the cash forecast. However, not all the figures come from this source. Dividends and corporation tax are just two examples of cash payments that affect the balance sheet but not the other budgets.

Non-cash items must be excluded from the cash budget, even though they are included in other budgets. For this reason it is usually not correct simply to transfer the bottom line from, for example, the different components of the revenue expenditure budget. The creation of a bad debt reserve and the depreciation charge are two examples of non-cash expenses that must be included in the expenditure budget but excluded from the cash budget.

It is extremely important that realistic timing assumptions are made when the cash budget is prepared. It is likely that few things will go into the cash budget at the same time that they go into the other budgets. Customers will take time to pay and you will take time to pay your suppliers. At this point a dangerous temptation should be mentioned. Suppose that the cash budget shows an unacceptable cash requirement on the bottom line. It can be tempting to 'solve' the problem by assuming that customers will pay more quickly and that suppliers will be paid more slowly. Unfortunately, writing it down does not make it happen. These assumptions should only be made if they are reasonable and, if necessary, action will be taken to support them.

An example of a cash budget form follows. The categories of receipts and expenses are for illustration purposes only and each business should use categories that suit its particular needs. It is necessary to calculate (or realistically assume) the opening bank balance, and many of the figures in the first one or two months will be derived from assumed transactions before the beginning of the budget period. The bottom line will go straight into the budgeted balance sheet.

Budgeted balance sheet

The budgeted balance sheet should be the last budget to be prepared. This is because everything in it is a consequence of the figures in one or more of the other budgets.

The balance sheet cannot be finalised until everything else has been finalised. The laws of bookkeeping dictate that every transaction affects two lines in the balance sheet. So, for example, paying the suppliers will reduce creditors and increase the bank overdraft.

The budgeted balance sheet should be laid out in monthly columns and the figures in the first column will be the anticipated balance sheet as at the start of the budget period. All the figures

Example of cash budget form

	January £000	February £000	March £000	April £000	May £000	June £000
Receipts						
UK customers						
Export customers						
Government grants						
All other						
Payments						
Suppliers						
Wages (net)						
PAYE and national insurance						
Corporation tax						
Dividends						
Capital expenditure						
All other						
Excess of receipts over payments						
Add opening bank balance						
Closing bank balance						

can be calculated mathematically from the figures in the other budgets. This will probably be done but it is not unknown for some short cuts to be taken, creditors being used as a balancing figure, for example. An example of a calculation is the following, which relates to the figure for fixed assets:

Opening balance
Plus capital expenditure   _____

Less depreciation   _____

Less disposals   _____

          _____

When the budgeted balance sheet has been finished, it is worth looking at it to see if any of the figures or trends seem unlikely. If they do, perhaps there is a fault in the logic of its preparation or perhaps one or more of the other budgets have some unlikely features and they are showing up in the balance sheet.

Should we bother with a budgeted balance sheet? Many managers do not, taking the view that it is sufficient to get a good profit budget and perhaps (or perhaps not) a good cash budget. I reject this view and believe that a budgeted balance sheet is valuable. For a start, it offers some assurance that the other budgets are complete and consistent. Managers should manage the balance sheet as well as the profit and loss account and a lending bank will probably be keen on it. Perhaps gearing, or one of the other ratios, will be seen to be unsatisfactory or even dangerous. It is as well to know.

Monitoring results against the budget

After the budget has been approved comes ... quite possibly not much or even nothing at all. This would be a pity but it would not mean that the budgeting exercise had been a complete waste of time. The participants will have thought logically about the organisation, its finances and its future. Some of the detail will remain lodged in their minds and influence their future actions. Nevertheless, it would be a pity, a great pity.

The budgets will be much more valuable if they are afterwards used to monitor what actually happens. Regular performance reports should be issued by the accountants. These should be in the same format as the budgets and should give, for appropriate categories, figures for the actual results alongside the equivalent budgets. Variances should also be given. It is normal to give the figures for a period (perhaps a month) and also for the year to date.

It is not normal to give all the reports to all the managers. Instead, distribution is usually done on a pyramid basis. The senior managers get most or all of the reports – perhaps in summarised form. The more junior managers get the reports for the departments that they manage. It sounds rigid and likely to offend the more junior managers, so perhaps some sensitivity on the point would not come amiss. The following is a good example of a budget variance report for one of the departments that make up the revenue expenditure budget.

	December month			December YTD		
	Budget	Actual	Variance	Budget	Actual	Variance
	£	£	£	£	£	£
Salaries	20,000	20,006	(6)	120,000	120,400	(400)
Commission	2,000	2,600	(600)	12,000	14,000	(2,000)
Pension costs	2,000	2,000	–	12,000	12,000	–
Car expenses	6,000	5,700	300	36,000	34,200	1,800
Other travel	1,000	900	100	6,000	5,100	900
Hotel expenses	3,000	3,250	(250)	18,000	21,700	(3,700)
Meals	1,000	995	5	6,000	5,870	130
Other expenses	1,000	1,400	(400)	6,000	6,100	(100)
Postage	200	190	10	1,200	1,160	40
Stationery	200	205	(5)	1,200	1,270	(70)
Telephone	2,000	2,150	(150)	12,000	11,900	100
Miscellaneous	1,000	930	70	6,000	5,200	800
	39,400	40,326	(926)	236,400	238,900	(2,500)

What happens when the budget variance reports are received? Perhaps nothing or not much – but something should. The purpose of the reports is to give managers the information to manage and deliver their budget commitments. More years ago than I care to remember, I regularly attended monthly meetings at Ford Motor Company's Thames Foundry in Dagenham. The plant manager had a rare talent for running a friendly, informal and very effective meeting to pick over the budget variance reports and organise corrective action where necessary. That is an example of what I mean.

Questions to test your understanding

Only two of these questions have a right answer. All the others are a matter of opinion. They are intended to make you think about your attitudes and the organisation for which you work. If you have done this, it is likely that your answers will be right for you.

1. Are budgets a waste of time?

2. What is the difference between a forecast and a budget?

3. Do you think that budgeted levels of achievement should be set:
   (a) Very easy?
   (b) Very difficult?
   (c) Somewhere in between?
   (d) According to some other system?

4. Do you think that budgeted levels of achievement in your organisation are too difficult? What changes (if any) should be made?

5. Do you think that the bottom-up method is better than the top-down method?

6. Are there likely to be any limiting factors in your organisation's budget? What are they? How might they be overcome?

7. What is your opinion of zero-based budgeting? Is it suitable for your organisation?

8. What is your opinion of flexible budgets? Are they suitable for your organisation?

9. Do you think that the budgeting process in your organisation could be improved? If so, how?

10. A late change is made to the capital expenditure budget. What other budget changes must be made as a consequence?

11. Sometimes departmental cost budgets consist only of costs that the managers can control. Sometimes head office or other costs that are beyond the managers' control are included. Which method do you prefer?

12. Do you think that a budgeted balance sheet should be prepared? If so, should it be available to all managers or just top managers?

13. This chapter includes an example of a budget variance report. Do you receive something similar to this and can you suggest any improvements?

INSTANT TIP

Arbitrary budget targets are de-motivating.

08

Is costing really mysterious?

The fact that the question in the title of this chapter is often asked indicates that many managers would instinctively answer 'yes'. This is a pity, because the principles of costing should not be too difficult to master. It is also a pity because businesses obviously need to control their costs and know exactly where in the business profits and losses are being made. Moreover, they need to set prices with reliable and useful costing information very much in mind. This chapter studies the following topics:

- Fixed and variable costs.
- Direct and indirect costs.
- The value of costing.
- The uses of costing.
- Recovering costs and internal charges.
- Absorption costing.
- Activity-based costing.
- Standard costing.
- Marginal costing.
- Break-even point and break-even charts.

- Selection of the most suitable costing method.
- Avoiding traps.

The chapter concludes with some questions for you to test your understanding.

Fixed and variable costs

An understanding of the differences between fixed and variable costs is of fundamental importance in any study of costing. Fixed costs do not vary according to the level of activity and a trivial example will illustrate the point. The filing fee to Companies House for a company's annual return is £15, if it is filed electronically. This fee does not vary according to the level of activity and it is the same amount whether the company's turnover is £10 or £10 million. Factory rent is a more substantial example of a fixed cost.

Variable costs, on the other hand, do vary according to the level of activity. An example is a company that buys goods for 50 pence and sells them for £1. The cost of the goods sold is variable and is proportionate to the sales. If twice as many goods are sold, the cost of sales is twice as much.

In practice, it is often not quite so straightforward. Some costs are really semi-variable and factory rent may be an example. It is only fixed up to the maximum level of production that can be achieved in the factory. Further sales, and consequently further production, must entail an increase in the cost. Perhaps it will be necessary to rent additional premises.

Direct and indirect costs

In some businesses, particularly manufacturing businesses, it may be useful to further divide costs into direct costs and the indirect costs closely associated with the cost of the product. This may be helpful in establishing the structure and detail of costs on which cost accounts are based. Such indirect costs are distinct from indirect costs not closely associated with the cost of the product. These may be termed overheads and include such things as advertising and the cost of running the accounts department.

In a manufacturing business, direct costs are often further divided into three categories:

- Direct labour.
- Direct materials.
- Direct other (electricity for machines etc.).

The total of these three categories is often called the prime cost.

Indirect production costs may include such things as quality control inspectors, factory heating etc. In a manufacturing business, prime cost plus these indirect costs equals the cost of manufacturing.

The value of costing

The value of costing can be illustrated with a simple example. Consider a company with three products. Its financial accounts show sales of £1 million, total costs of £700,000, and a profit of £300,000. The managers think that this is very good and that no significant changes are necessary. However, the cost accounts disclose the following:

	Product 1 (£000)	Product 2 (£000)	Product 3 (£000)	Total (£000)
Sales	600	300	100	1,000
Fixed costs	70	60	50	180
Variable costs	280	160	80	520
Total costs	350	220	130	700
Profit **contribution**	250	80	(30)	300

This shows that Product 1, as well as having the biggest proportion of sales, is contributing proportionately the most profit. Despite the overall good profit, Product 3 is making a negative contribution.

The obvious reaction might be to discontinue Product 3, but this may well be a mistake. £50,000 of fixed costs would have to be allocated to the other two products and the total profit would be reduced to £280,000. Product 3 should probably only be discontinued if the fixed costs can be cut, or if the other two products can be expanded to absorb the £50,000 fixed costs.

The uses of costing

It costs time and money to produce costing information and it is only worth doing if the information is put to good use. The following are some of the possible uses.

To control costs
Possession of detailed information about costs is of obvious value in the controlling of those costs.

To promote responsibility
Power and responsibility should go together, though often they do not. Timely and accurate costing information will help top management hold all levels of management responsible for the budgets that they control. Care should be taken that managers are not held responsible for costs that are not within their control. As you may know from bitter experience, this does sometimes happen.

To aid business decisions
The example concerning the company with three products given earlier in this chapter might be such a decision. Management must decide what to do about the unprofitable product.

To aid decisions on pricing

We live in competitive times and the old 'cost plus' contracts are now almost never encountered. What the market will bear is usually the main factor in setting prices. Nevertheless, detailed knowledge concerning costs should be an important factor in determining prices. Only in very exceptional circumstances should managers agree to price goods at below cost, and almost always they will seek to make an acceptable margin over cost. Accurate costing is vital when tenders are submitted for major contracts and errors can have significant consequences.

Cost information is, of course, provided to help the managers of the business and it is not often made available outside the business. It may be commercially valuable to competitors and for this reason it is usually kept secret.

Recovering costs and internal charges

It is very important that this is done sensibly, as mistakes will affect the results, though it may not be easy and some decisions will be a matter of opinion. It is usually not difficult to establish and allocate direct costs, but it is much more difficult to deal with the overheads.

The method normally adopted is to divide the business into separate cost centres. A cost centre is any location, function or item of equipment in respect of which costs may be ascertained and related to cost units for control purposes. Examples of the division of a business into cost centres may include a factory which is divisible into shops or departments, for example, welding shop, plating shop, assembly shop etc. Other examples could be each route covered by an airline or each department in a department store. Overheads are then listed and any internal charges are included in the figures for each category of overhead. The following is an example of what happens and how the figures are used:

	£
Property costs	200,000
Electricity	180,000
Management salaries	300,000
Canteen subsidy	60,000

There are three departments – welding, assembly and packing which have statistics as:

	Welding	Assembly	Packing
Floor area	900	600	500
No. of workers	40	80	30
Power usage of machinery	600	100	200

The second procedure is to apportion the overheads to the cost centres in accordance with some appropriate criteria. In this case these might be:

Overhead apportionment schedule

	Method	Total	Welding	Assembly	Packing
		£	£	£	£
Property costs	Floor area	200,000	90,000	60,000	50,000
Electricity	Power usage of machinery	180,000	120,000	20,000	40,000
Management	No. of workers	300,000	80,000	160,000	60,000
Canteen	No. of workers	60,000	16,000	32,000	12,000
		740,000	306,000	272,000	162,000

Absorption costing

Absorption costing takes all the costs and allocates them to particular products or cost centres. It is particularly useful for a manufacturing business but it can be used in a service business as well. It is necessary to take each cost and decide whether it is a direct cost or an indirect cost. The difference is:

- Direct costs clearly relate to a particular product or cost centre.
- Indirect costs relate to several products or cost centres.

This is best illustrated with an example:
Fruit Products manufactures three types of jam. Its overhead costs in January are £18,000 and it allocates them in the proportion of direct labour costs. The following details are available for January:

	Strawberry	*Raspberry*	*Apricot*	*Total*
Jars manufactured	*26,000*	*60,000*	*87,000*	*173,000*
Direct labour	*£2,000*	*£4,000*	*£6,000*	*£12,000*
Ingredients	*£6,000*	*£11,000*	*£17,000*	*£34,000*
Other direct costs	*£2,000*	*£3,000*	*£6,000*	*£11,000*

This leads to the following cost statement:

Fruit Products Ltd – January cost statement

	Strawberry	Raspberry	Apricot	Total
Jars produced	26,000	60,000	87,000	173,000
	£	£	£	£
Costs				
Direct labour	2,000	4,000	6,000	12,000
Ingredients	6,000	11,000	17,000	34,000
Other direct costs	2,000	3,000	6,000	11,000
Total direct costs	10,000	18,000	29,000	57,000
Overhead allocation	3,000	6,000	9,000	18,000
Total cost	13,000	24,000	38,000	75,000
Cost per Jar	50.0p	40.0p	43.7p	43.4p

You will notice that in the example, direct labour is smaller than the overhead cost that is being allocated. If the overheads had been allocated in a different way, perhaps on floor area utilised, then the result would almost certainly not have been the same.

The indirect costs must, in some fair way, be distributed over all the cost centres. They must be *absorbed* by the cost centres, which is why it is called *absorption costing*. Modern trends are for indirect costs to be a higher proportion of all costs. This means that the manner in which they are allocated is increasingly important. A change in the manner of allocating can have big results and may, for example, change a loss-making product or service into a profit-making product or service.

There is not a single correct method of allocating indirect costs to the individual cost centres and it is sometimes right to allocate different costs in different ways. The aim should be to achieve fairness in each individual case.

Among the costs that can be entirely allocated to individual cost centres are direct wages and associated employment costs, materials, and bought-in components. Among the costs that cannot be entirely allocated to individual cost centres are indirect wages (cleaners, maintenance staff etc.), wages of staff such as salesmen and accountants and general overheads such as property costs. Great care must be taken in deciding the best way to allocate the non-direct costs. There are many different ways and the following two are common examples.

Production hours

The overhead costs are apportioned according to the direct production hours charged to each product or cost centre. For example, consider a company with just two products, A having 5,000 hours charged and B having 10,000 hours charged. If the indirect costs are £60,000, product A will absorb £20,000 and product B will absorb £40,000.

Machine hours
The principle is the same but the overhead is allocated according to the number of hours that the machinery has been running.

Activity-based costing

Activity-based costing has many similarities to absorption costing. The difference is that the way that overheads are allocated to products or cost centres is different. If absorption costing is used, the overheads are allocated according to volume. If activity-based costing is used, the overheads are allocated according to *specific activities carried on by the business.*

Activity-based costing has the disadvantage that it is more complicated and difficult to manage. However, the results may well be more useful. High-volume or standardised products or services attract more overheads in absorption costing systems than under activity-based costing principles. On the other hand, short-run 'one-off' products and services attract less, even though they often generate more support and overhead costs.

Standard costing

Standard costing can be closely linked to budgetary control. It is very useful for controlling costs, monitoring performance against budgets and identifying the exact reasons (good and bad) why performance differs from budgets or standards. An essential step is to set the targets, or standards, for the different factors affecting costs. Actual results can then be compared with the standards. This should show how the overall result compared with the overall standard and also how each of the factors contributed to the result. It is best illustrated with a very simple example.

A manufacturer of linen handkerchiefs sells to wholesalers in bundles each containing 100 handkerchiefs. The following standards are set for the month of July:

Standard linen usage per bundle	*54 square metres*
Standard linen price	*£0.30 per metre*
Actual number of bundles produced	*20,000*
Actual amount of linen used	*1,220,000 square metres*
Actual cost of linen used	*£317,200*

This is, of course, a very simplified example but the following conclusions can be drawn.

Material price variance
Standard price (1,220,000 × £0.30)	£366,000
Actual price	£317,200
Favourable variance	£48,800

The favourable price variance is 13.3 per cent.

Material usage variance
Standard usage (20,000 × 54 metres)	1,080,000 metres
Actual usage	1,220,000 metres
	140,000 metres

Unfavourable variance (measured to the designed amount – not the end result) is 140,000 metres × £0.30 = £52,000.
This is 13.0 per cent.

Marginal costing

Absorption costing results in all costs (fixed and variable) being included in the costs. Marginal costing concentrates very heavily on marginal costs and excludes fixed costs. This often provides very useful information for pricing and other management decisions. Marginal costing can be defined as: '*The change in cost which occurs when the volume of output is increased or reduced by one unit.*'

It is essential that the costs be split between fixed and variable, though this might in practice be difficult and some costs may be semi-variable. The following is an illustration of marginal costing in a single-product business:

	Total	Fixed	Variable
	£	£	£
Sales (60,000 units)	300,000		
Costs	250,000	150,000	100,000
Net profit	50,000		

The following shows the figures in a form useful for marginal costing:

	Unit basis	
	£	£
Sales (60,000 units)	300,000	5.00
Less variable costs	100,000	1.66
Contribution	200,000	3.34
Less fixed costs	150,000	2.50
Net profit	50,000	0.84

This means that for every one unit increase in sales there will be extra revenue of £5.00 and an extra contribution of £3.34. As fixed costs will not change, the net profit will also increase by £3.34. If additional sales are made at a unit price of £3.35, there will be an increase in the overall profit. When the marginal costs are low, the reward for achieving extra sales is high, and when the marginal costs are high, there is less incentive to achieve extra sales. This is one reason why cruises are heavily discounted to prevent the ship sailing half empty. The fixed costs of a cruise ship are high and, for example, the fuel cost of the ship will be virtually the same, whether it is full or not.

Break-even point and break-even charts

Break-even point occurs when the costs exactly equal the revenues. At break-even point there is neither a profit or loss. A break-even chart can show at what level of sales break-even point is achieved. Furthermore, it can show the level of profit or loss at any particular level of sales. In order to do this, it is necessary to know:

- the amount of fixed costs;
- the amount of variable costs per unit of sale;
- the sales price per unit.

In practice, it may be very difficult or impossible to identify all the factors accurately. Some costs may be semi-variable and fixed costs may increase once a certain level of sales is reached. Various other problems may be encountered. The principles are illustrated with a very simple example.

A club is planning a dance for its members. Tickets will be sold for £30 each. The fixed costs (band and hire of hall) will be £1,500. The variable costs (food etc.) will be £10 per ticket sold.

Each ticket makes a contribution of £20 (£30 less £10) towards the fixed costs. After the fixed costs have been recovered each ticket sold will make a profit of £20.

The vertical axis represents the costs.
The horizontal axis represents the number of tickets sold.
Line A – B is the fixed costs of £1,500.
Line C – D is the total revenue at £30 per ticket.
Line A – E is the total costs of £10 per ticket plus the fixed costs.
The break-even point is where line A – E crosses with line C – D. The dotted line downwards shows that this happens when 75 tickets are

sold. Revenue is £2,250 (75 x £30). Total costs are £2,250 (75 x £10 plus fixed costs of £1,500). If only 74 tickets are sold, there will be a £20 loss. If 76 tickets are sold, there will be a £20 profit.

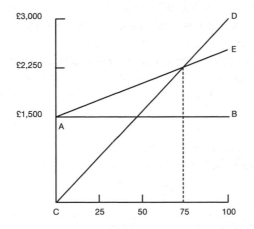

This break-even chart could not be more simple but exactly the same principles can be applied to a business situation. The following example illustrates this.

A company imports and sells clocks. It pays £5 for each clock and the selling price per clock is £10. The company has fixed costs of £200,000.

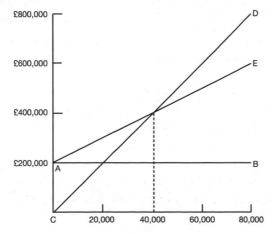

The vertical axis represents the costs.
The horizontal axis represents the number of clocks sold.
Line A – B is the fixed costs of £200,000.
Line C – D is the total sales at £10 per clock.
Line A – E is the total costs at £5 per clock plus the fixed costs.

The break-even point is the sale of 40,000 clocks. At this point sales of £400,000 is equal to fixed costs of £200,000 plus the cost of 40,000 clocks at £5 each. The difference between lines C – D and A – E is the profit or loss.

Selection of the most suitable costing method

All the costing systems have advantages and disadvantages. The following are some of the factors that should be considered.

Standard costing
This is very useful when reliable budgets and pre-set standards are in place. As it measures actual costs against standard costs, it is very good for controlling costs and enabling managers to correct deviations from budgets or standards. Standard costing is not a stand-alone costing technique and it can be used in conjunction with all the other methods.

Absorption costing
This is possibly the most complete of the costing systems because every cost is absorbed into the costs. It is advantageous when managers want to do this. It makes it very difficult to forget or ignore certain costs.

Activity-based costing
This has the advantages of absorption costing but overheads are allocated according to activity rather than volume. This is more

sophisticated and may be more suitable in some cases.

Marginal costing
This is very useful for making management decisions, particularly relating to pricing. As it concentrates on marginal costs to the exclusion of fixed costs, it helps managers concentrate on key marginal factors.

Avoiding traps
There are quite a lot of possible traps. They include the following.

Selecting unsuitable costing techniques
Several costing methods are described in this chapter and there are others that are not included. There are also variations on the methods. Businesses should select the ones that best suit their needs.

Misunderstanding of marginal costing
Marginal costing is a very useful management tool for various reasons. In particular, it enables managers to make intelligent pricing decisions. However, managers should remember that there are dangers in not absorbing overheads or fixed costs, particularly as very competitively priced orders may be easy to obtain. Unless all the fixed costs are covered by total sales, an overall loss will result.

Misallocation between fixed costs and variable costs
This could have unfortunate results and there may be difficulties in practice. Some costs are really semi-variable. For example, suppose that the maximum output of a factory is 100,000 units per month and that this figure cannot be increased without considerable expenditure. If an order is accepted that requires factory output of 103,000 units a month, expenditure to increase the capacity of the factory will be necessary. It would be a bad mistake to overlook this.

Allocation of costs to wrong cost centres
This will obviously cause problems and a single mistake will cause errors in two cost centres.

Slowness in getting the figures
Delay can be a problem with all forms of accounting, including cost accounting. Management may make bad decisions based on out of date information. It may be better to have quick information that is 95 per cent reliable than slow information that is 100 per cent reliable.

Unfair internal charges
In many businesses certain departments make charges to certain other departments. This is normally for very good reasons but it is essential that the charges are fair and seen to be fair, especially if the department charged has no say in the matter and is forbidden to purchase elsewhere. Operational managers often resent internal charges imposed by head office, especially if the decisions are made by head office managers.

Managers made responsible for costs that they cannot control
This always demotivates.

Questions to test your understanding

1. Relating to absorption costing
Salzburg Airlines is a small airline based at Salzburg in Austria. It operates just two routes – to Budapest and to Warsaw. It does its accounting in dollars.

In April the Budapest route takes $300,000 revenue and planes are in the air for 200 hours. Direct costs (pilots' wages etc.) are $110,000.

In April the Warsaw route takes $430,000 revenue and planes are in the air for 250 hours. Direct costs (pilots' wages etc.) are $160,000.

Indirect costs (rent of space at airport terminal etc.) total $360,000. These costs should be allocated in the proportion of hours in the air.

Please prepare the cost statement for April. Do you think that profits would increase if the least profitable route were to be shut down?

2. Relating to standard costing

A supplier of chauffer-driven cars sets the following standards for the month of July:

Driver's employment costs per kilometre	£0.40
Vehicle costs per kilometre	£0.20
Standard charge to customers per kilometre	£0.80

The actual figures for the month of July are:

Actual number of kilometres charged	3,000
Actual employment costs of driver	£1,300
Actual vehicle costs	£700
Total amount charged to customers	£2,500

Please calculate three useful variances.

3. Question relating to marginal costing

Using the data given in the section on marginal costing please prepare a cost statement assuming that 61,000 units are sold instead of 60,000 units.

4. Question relating to break-even point and break-even chart

A contract cleaning business charges £12 per hour to supply its services. Its fixed costs are £50,000 per month. Its variable costs are £8 for each chargeable hour to customers.

1. Please prepare a break-even chart.

2. How many hours must be charged to customers in order for the business to break-even?

3. How many hours must be charged to customers for the business to make a profit of £4,000?

INSTANT TIP

A thorough understanding of the differences between fixed costs and variable costs is important in all forms of costing.

09

What should I know about financial difficulties and insolvency?

Important points about this chapter

Much of this chapter deals with the law and it is the law of England and Wales. Due to space considerations it has been necessary to greatly summarise and simplify some of the legal points and processes.

This is probably the most ambitious and wide-ranging part of the book, its aim being to give some useful knowledge of a number of topics embraced by the title of the chapter. It is very much to be hoped that it will be of academic interest only and that you will never need to use it, but it is only being realistic to acknowledge that you might. In any case, it might be useful if one of your customers experiences financial difficulties.

An obvious but sometimes overlooked point is that prevention is better than cure. Businesses should be soundly financed and run in a way that minimises the risks of financial difficulties and insolvency. If your business is not being run in this way, perhaps you should speak up – even if it makes you unpopular.

The chapter starts with the role and responsibilities of directors, including the personal risks that they may run. If you are a director as well as a manager, you should certainly know all about them. If this is not the case, it is probably still a good idea to have this knowledge. You may need to give advice and perhaps you will be a director soon. The two topics studied are:

- Directors' responsibilities when they believe that a company may have financial difficulties.
- Personal risks for directors when a company experiences financial difficulties.

A company experiencing financial difficulties may go into administration, which is not the same as insolvency or liquidation. In fact, the first aim of administration is to save all, or at least part, of the company. This does sometimes happen, but sadly not always. Administration may be frustrating for the creditors but it is for their benefit. The three aspects of administration considered are:

- The concept of administration.
- The objectives of administration.
- Administration: the moratorium.

The next area covered is how companies (and also unincorporated businesses) end their existence and, most importantly, in the case of an insolvent winding-up the rules governing how any available money is distributed among the creditors. The topics covered are:

- The three ways that companies may be wound up.
- The two ways that companies may be struck off.

- Priority of distribution of funds in a winding-up.
- The insolvency of an unincorporated business.
- Bankruptcy.

The final subject is bad debts and this is considered in three areas as follows:

- Definition of a bad debt.
- Tax consequences of a bad debt.
- Bad debts: practical considerations.

The chapter concludes with some questions for you to test your understanding.

Directors' responsibilities when they believe that a company may have financial difficulties

Directors should, of course, do their best to ensure that financial difficulties do not happen. However, it is only being realistic to recognise that problems will sometimes occur in some companies. When they do, the role of the directors is extremely important. This is both to make the best of the situation for the creditors and the company itself, and also to protect their own positions. If the financial difficulties are serious, the directors' first duty is to the creditors as a whole rather than to the members as a whole.

Directors are required to keep proper records and accounts. This is always important, but it is especially important if financial difficulties are experienced. Good records and accounts should give early warning of impending trouble and they should give the facts on which a plan of action can be based.

The courts recognise that the directors of small private companies may not have the same expertise as the directors of large companies. They may be more tolerant in the case of their failings. Nevertheless, there are minimum standards expected of all directors. All directors should keep proper accounts or pay someone to do it, and they should review the figures. If problems are indicated, they should do the necessary investigations and projections. If they do not do it themselves, they should commission someone with the necessary expertise.

An extremely important point is that they should usually take independent professional advice and they should do so quickly. This should be from a person able to give such advice, very probably a suitably qualified accountant or solicitor. It is possible that the advice will be taken from a licensed insolvency practitioner or that they will be advised to speak to a licensed insolvency practitioner.

What happens afterwards depends on the advice that is given. Some of the possibilities are:

1. They could decide (after taking advice) to carry on trading. It may be necessary to explain the problems and the plan to the bank and/or creditors.

2. They could decide to put the company into administration.

3. They could decide to seek an injection of capital.

4. They could decide to seek an amalgamation or reconstruction.

5. They could decide to recommend to the members that the company be voluntarily wound up.

6. They could accept that the company must be compulsorily wound up.

There are real risks for the directors personally and these are detailed in the next section. There are two dangers in particular of which they should be aware:

1. They should not carry on trading beyond the point at which trading should stop.

2. They should not exercise undue preference and especially they should not make payments that unduly prefer their own interests. An example would be to pay off a bank overdraft against which directors' personal guarantees have been given.

There can be great pressure on directors when a company faces financial difficulties. It sometimes happens that directors put all their energies into 'fire fighting' and such things as boosting sales and fending off creditors. This can be tempting and it may work, in which case they will be the heroes. However, they should not neglect the accounts and their responsibilities. Above all they should seek professional advice.

Personal risks for directors when a company experiences financial difficulties

One or more of the directors may face personal risks in one or more of five areas:

1. Personal liability for wrongful trading
This can happen when a company is liquidated and there is not enough money to pay all creditors in full. A court may order one or more directors to make a contribution to the deficiency. This may be done if a director knew or ought to have known that an insolvent liquidation was likely, but failed to stop trading or failed to take reasonable steps to minimise the deficiency.

2. Disqualification
A director may be disqualified by a court from holding the position of director in any company.

3. Criminal liability
This can happen if a director breaks one of several laws and in particular is guilty of fraudulent trading. Fraudulent trading can take place even if a company does not go into liquidation.

4. Personal liability for fraudulent trading
A director guilty of fraudulent trading may be ordered to contribute in the case of winding up. This can only happen if the company is wound up.

5. Misfeasance
This does not necessarily involve dishonesty, although it may do so. It does involve the wrongful direction or detention of company assets. It may include, for example, paying a dividend out of capital and it may include a director purchasing company assets at a price below their true value.

The concept of administration

Prior to the implementation of the Insolvency Act 1986, British law did not offer companies the possibility of a period of protection from the pressure of creditors. Companies went into liquidation that might have been saved and turned round, and companies failed totally when parts of them might have been saved. Jobs were lost and creditors lost money in circumstances where this might have been preventable. Many countries did have laws that offered a breathing space to companies in trouble. In particular, the USA had laws that gave a period of protection. The Insolvency Act 1986 introduced the concept of a period of protection, which was influenced by American law and experience, although UK law is very different.

Subject to rules and safeguards, the directors may put a company into administration and there are various ways in which this can be done. Administration takes control of a company away from the directors and puts it into the hands of an administrator who must be a licensed insolvency practitioner. Administration must be conducted with the purpose of achieving a stated objective and details of this are given next in this chapter. Whilst a company is in administration, it has a large degree of protection from its creditors.

At the termination of the administration control is passed back to the directors. If a liquidator has been appointed, control is passed to them instead of the directors.

The objectives of administration

There are three permitted objectives:

1. Rescue the company as a going concern.

2. Achieve a better result for the company's creditors as a whole than would be likely if the company were to be wound up (without first being in administration).

3. Realise property in order to make a distribution to one or more secured or preferential creditors.

The administrator will be required to pursue the first objective so long as they think it reasonably practical to do so. Rescuing the company as a going concern means the company and as much of its business as possible.

Only if the administrator believes that it is not reasonably practical to rescue the company as a going concern may they pursue the second objective.

Only if the administrator believes that it is not reasonably practical to pursue either of the first two objectives may they pursue the third objective. The administrator must have regard to the interests of all creditors. In situations where there are insufficient funds to pay the unsecured creditors, the administrator may only pursue the third objective if it does not unnecessarily harm the interests of the unsecured creditors.

Administration: the moratorium

An essential feature of administration is that the company has a period of protection from its creditors. This is known as the moratorium. The effects of the moratorium include the following:

1. No order may be passed for the winding-up of the company except a petition in the public interest or a petition by the Financial Services Authority.

2. No resolution may be passed for the winding-up of the company. This covers both a members' voluntary liquidation and a creditors' voluntary liquidation.

3. The following may not happen except with the permission of the court or the agreement of the administrator:
   (a) No step may be taken to repossess property subject to a hire purchase agreement.
   (b) No step may be taken to enforce security over the company's property.
   (c) A landlord may not exercise the right of forfeiture by peaceable re-entry.
   (d) No legal process may be commenced or continued against the company or its property.
   (e) Goods may not be repossessed under the authority of a retention of title clause in the conditions of sale.

The three ways that companies may be wound up

The three ways that a company may be wound up are: members' voluntary winding-up; creditors' voluntary winding-up; and winding-up by the court.

Members' voluntary winding-up

This is done following a decision of the members, which in most cases means the shareholders. The members can decide to do this for any reason that they consider sound. It can only be done in this way if the company is solvent and the creditors will be paid in full. As this chapter is about financial difficulties and insolvency, nothing more needs to be said.

Creditors' voluntary winding-up

This too is done following a decision of the members, which in most cases means the shareholders. It is a creditors' voluntary winding-up when the company is insolvent and it is believed that not all the creditors will be paid in full. The creditors are in charge of the winding-up. The members resolve that the company be wound up and make a provisional appointment of the liquidator. At a subsequent creditors' meeting the creditors may confirm this appointment or substitute their own choice of liquidator. The liquidator will realise the assets and pay the creditors in the order of precedence prescribed by law.

At the end of the process the liquidator will send final accounts and a statement to the members, the creditors and to the registrar of companies. Three months after this has been done, the company will be dissolved and it will cease to exist.

Winding-up by the court

If this happens, the winding-up is not the choice of the members. It is a decision made by the court over the heads of the members. There are a number of reasons why the court might do this but by far the most common is because it has received evidence that a creditor owed more than £750 has served a statutory demand on the company and that payment has not been made in a period of at least three weeks.

The procedure for a winding-up by the court is as follows:

1. The petition will be heard by the court, which may accept it and issue a winding-up order.

2. The Official Receiver becomes the liquidator and the directors are relieved of their powers.

3. The directors must prepare a statement of affairs within 21 days.

4. The Official Receiver may call a meeting of creditors which will appoint a liquidator to take over from him. Alternatively, the Official Receiver may proceed with the liquidation himself and not call a meeting of creditors.

5. The liquidator realises the assets and pays the creditors in the order of precedence prescribed by law.

6. At the end of the process the company is dissolved and ceases to exist.

The two ways that companies may be struck off

A company may be struck off following an application by the directors. It must not have traded or changed its name within the previous three months and there are a few other restrictions too. There is a £10 fee and any remaining assets pass to the Crown. This is the quick, cheap and simple way to dispose of an unwanted dormant, solvent company.

The Registrar of Companies may strike off a company if he believes that the company is no longer in business or operation. He usually forms this opinion because it stops submitting accounts and annual returns, and because it does not respond to communications and warnings from him. After warnings to the company and its directors, and after advertising her intention by other means, he will eventually strike off the company and it will be dissolved.

The fact that the company has been struck off will not release the company and its officers from their obligations. This may include obligations to pay fines and civil penalties. If the company is still in business or operation, it may apply to be restored to the register. This inevitably involves difficulty and expense.

Priority of distribution of funds in a winding-up

The holder of a fixed charge gets paid out of the proceeds of their security. If the security does not realise enough to pay them in full, they may rank as creditors for the remainder of the debt. If the security realises more than enough to pay them in full, the surplus is available for the other creditors. The order of priority is as follows:

1. The expenses of the liquidation (this includes the liquidator's fees).
2. Preferential debts (but not interest due after the liquidation).
3. Debts secured by a qualifying floating charge (but not interest due after the liquidation).
4. Ordinary debts (but not interest due after the liquidation).
5. Interest on preferential and ordinary debts at the statutory rate.
6. The contributors (members).

If the contributors get anything the business was not insolvent.

Each category is paid in full before funds become available for the next category. If funds are not sufficient to pay a category in full, a pro rata payment is made. For example, suppose that ordinary debts total £100,000 and that only £50,000 is available. Each debt is paid at the rate of 50p in the pound.

Preferential debts (which rank equally between themselves) are:

1. Contributions to occupational pension schemes etc. – up to four months in arrears and without a monetary limit.

2. Remuneration etc. of employees – up to four months in arrears and not exceeding £800.

3. Levies on coal and steel production.

4. Money owing to third parties in connection with debts, which would have been preferential had they not been paid by the third parties.

The insolvency of an unincorporated business

An unincorporated business may be a sole trader or a general partnership in which the partners have joint and several liability. A company will cease to exist if it is wound up or struck off, but there is no corresponding process for an unincorporated business. It is, however, unless there are clear lines of financial support, required to stop trading.

If the debts cannot be paid in full, the net assets are applied in a way similar to what happens in an insolvent company. A sole trader is personally responsible for the debts up to and including bankruptcy. The partners in a general partnership each have personal joint and several personal liability for the debts up to and including bankruptcy.

Bankruptcy

Bankruptcy has obvious parallels with the winding-up of an insolvent company. A key difference is that at the end of the process the company is dissolved and ceases to exist. A bankrupt person still exists and must get on with the rest of their life. The process of bankruptcy starts with the presentation of a bankruptcy petition to the court. This may be done by the person themselves or by an unpaid creditor or judgment creditor. The amount owing must be at least £750. If the petition is brought by a creditor, a statutory demand must first have been sent to the debtor.

The petition is advertised in the *London Gazette* or the *Edinburgh Gazette.* It is then heard by the court, which may issue a bankruptcy order if it is right to do so. When a bankruptcy order has been issued, the Official Receiver becomes the bankrupt's trustee in bankruptcy. The trustee will proceed to realise the assets of the bankrupt. Ultimately, the proceeds will be distributed to creditors. The order of priority is the same as for the distribution relating to a company.

The bankrupt is permitted to retain certain property. This includes personal clothes, bedding and the necessaries of life. They are also permitted to retain the tools of their trade. It will depend on individual circumstances, but the definition of this might be quite widely drawn. For example, as well as tools it might include such things as a computer or a van. An undischarged bankrupt must operate under certain restrictions. They may not, for example, be a director of a company, and may not obtain credit without disclosing they are an undischarged bankrupt. In most cases, they are automatically discharged from bankruptcy in a maximum of a year, though this does not apply in certain circumstances.

Definition of a bad debt

The perception of the public is that a bad debt happens when a customer goes bust, but this definition is inadequate and seriously flawed. A much better definition is that a bad debt occurs when either a customer cannot pay or will not pay and the supplier is unable or unwilling to take the necessary steps to force them to pay.

If a customer is unable to pay, the debt must ultimately be written off as a bad debt. This must be done whether or not the customer is formally declared insolvent. If a customer can pay but will not do so, steps must ultimately be taken to force them to do so. If a supplier is unable or unwilling to take these steps, the debt must be written off. A bad debt should not be confused with a credit note raised for some other reason. It may, for example, be decided to credit a customer for reasons of goodwill or because of a genuine dispute.

Tax consequences of a bad debt

It should always be possible to gain relief against corporation tax, if the supplier that suffers the bad debt pays corporation tax. Similarly, it should always be possible to gain relief against income tax, if the supplier that suffers the bad debt pays income tax. In both cases it is assumed that the bad debt relates to a transaction for profit on which the appropriate tax is payable. Corporation tax relief or income tax relief is at the top marginal rate.

VAT bad debt relief is available when an invoice has been unpaid for six months and is fully written off in the books of the supplier. It is sufficient for the full write-off to be in the internal accounts and it is not necessary to wait until the write-off is in the signed, statutory accounts. However, the statutory accounts must of course, ultimately include the write-off. The write-off must be specific and a general provision will not do.

The recovery may be effected by claiming in the next VAT return after these conditions are satisfied. If any money is subsequently recovered from the customer, the appropriate VAT part must be declared and paid to HM Revenue and Customs. All this applies to most businesses but, of course, a business that pays VAT on a cash receipts basis will not have paid over the VAT in the first place.

Bad debts: practical considerations

If a customer can pay but will not do so, the supplier must take some policy decisions about how far it is sensible to pursue the debt. If the case is good, judgment in the supplier's favour should be obtained. In practice, many customers make payment when faced with the credible threat of imminent legal action. More make payment as soon as the threat is put into practice. Still more do not defend the claim and judgment by default is obtainable.

It may be possible to invoke a retention of title clause in the supplier's conditions of sale, if one exists and if it is legally enforceable. This, of course, is only applicable if physical goods have been supplied. Services cannot be repossessed.

Interest on late payment may be included in the terms of a contract. If this is the case and if it has not already been charged, interest should be billed up to date. It may be possible to charge statutory interest.

It sometimes happens that not every last penny that is contractually chargeable has actually been charged. This may be for various reasons including goodwill, but if the supplier is faced with a bad debt, goodwill is probably no longer a consideration. Consideration should be given to raising invoices and it should be possible to go right back to the point where such debts become statute-barred. This is five years for Scotland and six years for the rest of the UK. Needless to say, such late billing should only be considered where there is a legal and contractual right to do so. Anything else would be dishonest.

The raising of legitimate further invoices should increase the amount ultimately received, even if the customer is insolvent. This is because if a dividend of x pence in the pound is ultimately paid, the sum on which it is calculated should be greater.

Questions to test your understanding

1. What is the first objective that an administrator must try to achieve if it is possible?

2. A customer has gone into administration. Can you recover goods under the authority of a retention of title clause in the conditions of sale?

3. In an insolvent winding-up does payment of the liquidator's fees rank ahead of the preferential creditors?

4. Your employer has gone into insolvent liquidation and you are owed one month's wages of £4,000. How much of this will rank as a preferential debt?

INSTANT TIP

In the matter of financial difficulties prevention is better than cure.

What else should I know?

This final chapter deals with seven unrelated topics that do not fit naturally into any of the other chapters. They are:

- Share capital, shares and dividends.
- Debentures.
- Pay As You Earn (PAYE).
- National insurance.
- Value Added Tax.
- Factoring of debts.

The chapter concludes with some questions for you to test your understanding.

Share capital, shares and dividends

Approximately four per cent of British companies are limited by guarantee and have no shares or shareholders. The remaining 96 per cent of companies have share capital, shareholders and the possibility of dividends. Most non-financial managers reading this book will work for a company having a share capital and it is worth explaining some relevant terms.

Authorised share capital

Prior to the implementation of the Companies Act 2006 it is compulsory for a company's memorandum to state the value of shares that can be issued, whether they have been or not. Either the memorandum or the articles must state how the authorised share capital is divided into shares of a different value and class. Shares may not be issued in excess of the authorised limit but it is fairly simple to have it raised. The Companies Act 2006, when implemented, makes authorised share capital voluntary, but for a long time it will apply in most companies.

Issued share capital

This is the part of the authorised share capital that has actually been issued.

Preference shares

These normally have a right to receive a dividend (either a fixed percentage or calculated in a specified way) that ranks before the rights of ordinary shares. There may be more than one class of preference share, with the rights of one ranking before the rights of another. The rights to receive a dividend may be cumulative, which means that a missed dividend is made up later if distributable profits become available. If the shares are non-cumulative, a missed dividend is permanently lost. Preference shares frequently, but not always, carry preferential rights to the return of capital in the event of the company being wound up. Such rights rank behind those of creditors, but ahead of those of ordinary shares.

Ordinary shares

If there is only one class of share, then the shares are ordinary shares. They may be described simply as 'shares' as there is no need to differentiate them from other shares. Ordinary shares rank behind preference shares in the right to receive dividends. They are highly geared compared with preference shares. If distributable profits are £600,000 and the preference shares have rights to a dividend of £500,000, the ordinary shares 'own' £100,000. If distributable profits rise to £2 million, the preference shares will still receive a dividend of £500,000. The same ordinary shares will then 'own' £1.5 million.

Ordinary shares rank behind creditors, and normally behind preference shares, in the event of the company being wound up. If there is insufficient money to pay the ordinary shareholders in full, they suffer the shortage. If there is a surplus, they share it between them. The holders of ordinary shares have full rights as to attendance and voting at meetings, and in the general governance of the company.

Share premium

It sometimes happens that a share is issued at a price higher than its nominal value. For example, a £1.00 share may be issued at a price of £1.10. In this case £1.00 is share capital and 10 pence is the share premium. Companies are restricted in what they can do with a share premium account.

Dividends must not be paid out of capital. They may only be paid out of net distributable realised profits, either made in the current year or retained from previous years. It is an important distinction which directors must observe. The Companies Act defines net distributable realised profits as follows:

> '... a company's profits available for distribution are its accumulated, realised profits, so far as not previously utilised by distribution or capitalisation, less its accumulated, realised losses, so far as not previously written off in a reduction or reorganisation of capital duly made.'

It is a serious matter to get it wrong. Non-financial managers are unlikely to be involved in dividend decisions, but non-financial directors will be.

One or more interim dividends may be declared and paid by the directors. A final dividend is proposed by the directors but must be sanctioned by the shareholders. In listed companies, subject to the money being available, interim and final dividends tend to follow predictable dates and amounts, hopefully showing a rising trend.

Debentures

Technically, a debenture is a document which acknowledges or creates a debt and promises repayment, with or without encompassing a charge or mortgage on one or more assets as security for it. In practice a charge or mortgage is virtually always an essential feature of it.

Some companies obtain finance by issuing a series of registered debentures. A lender takes a debenture as security and receives interest on it. The lender is not a shareholder and does not own any part of the company. Instead, the loan is secured by a charge on some or all of the assets of the company.

Debentures are also a standard form of security for bank and other lending. They give the holder (or lender) a fixed or floating charge (or both) over the assets of the company. Charges must be registered at Companies House and the holder's priority is jeopardised if this is not done. It is possible to create more than one charge on the same assets. If this is done, the priority of the charges is determined by the order in which they are registered.

Bank overdrafts are usually repayable on demand and the words mean exactly what they say. A bank may take steps to enforce its security if repayment is not made on demand. Banks have in the past been criticised for being too quick to enforce their security but it is generally recognised that they are now much less likely to act prematurely. Long-term lending secured by a debenture is only repayable early if the covenants are breached.

A fixed charge relates to a specific identified asset or specified assets. These assets are the security of the debenture holders and the directors are forbidden to dispose of them. They will probably also be required to insure them and maintain them in good order. Disposal may only be with the permission of the debenture holder or trustee. A floating charge relates to all the assets of the company. Directors are allowed to buy and sell assets subject to a floating charge, so long as it is done in the normal course of business for the benefit of the company. The terms of a floating charge usually prevent a fixed charge being created to rank ahead of the floating charge. But it is allowed if they do not do so.

Pay As You Earn (PAYE)

Employers are required by law to operate the PAYE system. Under it, income tax and national insurance contributions are deducted at source from the pay of employees and paid over to HM Revenue and Customs (HMRC). PAYE works by the Revenue giving a code to the employer and this must be used in working out the income tax deduction. It works, using the rates and allowances for 2007–08, as follows:

Allowances	**£**
Personal allowance	5,225
Job expenses	65
	5,290
Pay deductions	
Car benefit	2,100
Part time earnings	990
Untaxed interest	200
	3,290

Tax-free pay for the year is £2,000 (£5,290 less £3,290). The last figure is taken away and a letter added to give the tax code 200L. The letter L signifies that the employee receives the basic personal allowance. There are a number of other letters used and two examples are:

P indicates the full personal allowance for a person aged between 65 and 74.

BR indicates tax deducted at the basic rate.

In the above example, and ignoring the pence, if the employee earns £25,000 a year and using current tax rates, the annual tax deducted by the employer will be.

Pay	£25,000
Less tax free amount for the year	£2,000
	£23,000
10 per cent of £2,230 =	£223
22 per cent of £20,770 =	£4,569
	£4,792

If the employee is paid monthly, one-twelfth of the tax (£399.33) will be deducted from each monthly payment.

National insurance

National insurance contributions are a compulsory charge on earnings from employment and the profits of the self-employed. The original concept was (and the theory still is) that these contributions will pay for the payment of national insurance benefits, but in practice the amount received by the state is significantly less than the cost of the benefits. Many people believe that the term 'national insurance' is really a misnomer and that the payments are really a special sort of income tax. The different classes of national insurance contributions are as follows.

Class 1 contributions

These are paid by employees unless they are over the retirement age. Contributions are only payable if the employee earns more than a specified amount and there is an upper limit above which contributions are not payable.

Employees pay 11 per cent on earnings between the lower and upper limits.

In addition to the contributions paid by employees, employers are required to pay contributions. These are 12.8 per cent on all earnings above the lower limit and without an upper limit.

Class 1A contributions

These apply to most benefits-in-kind. They are paid only by the employer and are a tax-deductible expense. They are not payable by employees.

Class 2 contributions

These are flat rate contributions paid by the self-employed. The amount is modest and at the time of writing the amount is slightly more than £2 per week. The contributions are only payable if earnings are not less than a specified annual sum.

Class 3 contributions

These are a type of voluntary contribution. A person who is neither employed nor self-employed, or who earns less than the exemption amount, may pay these contributions to secure the state retirement pension.

Class 4 contributions

These are payable by the self-employed as a percentage of their profits as determined for income tax purposes. The rate is 8 per cent between a lower earnings limit and an upper earning limit, and 1 per cent above the upper earnings limit.

Value Added Tax

Value Added Tax (or VAT) is delightfully simple in concept, which was one of its attractions when it was introduced into the UK in 1973. It replaced purchase tax and selective employment tax and was a commitment on joining the European Economic Community, which has since transmogrified into the European Union. Despite the simplicity of the concept, it is horribly complicated in practice.

VAT is an indirect tax on consumer expenditure, charged on business transactions and on imports. VAT charged by a business is paid to HM Revenue and Customs, but VAT paid by the business is deducted from the payment. This continues until a purchase is made by a consumer who pays the tax and recovers nothing. It is best illustrated with an example.

Manufacturer A makes a product and sells it for £100 plus 17.5 per cent VAT to Wholesaler B. Manufacturer A pays £17.50 to HMRC, but may deduct the VAT that it has paid to its suppliers.

Wholesaler B sells the product for £130.00 plus 17.5 per cent VAT (£22.75) to Retailer C. Wholesaler B pays £5.25 (£22.75 less £17.50) to HMRC.

Retailer C sells the product for £200.00 plus 17.5 per cent VAT (£35.00) to Mrs Smith. Retailer C pays £12.25 (£35 less £22.75) to HMRC.

Mrs Smith has paid £235.00 for the product and recovers nothing.

Her Majesty's government has received £35 and spends it wisely for the benefit of the citizens of the country.

Registration for VAT is compulsory when a business's turnover reaches the specified annual threshold. A business may choose to register for VAT even though its turnover is below the threshold. This can be an advantage because VAT paid out can be recovered, and although VAT must be added to sales, a VAT-registered customer can recover it. If its customers are not registered for VAT, it is probably not a good idea because the sales will be effectively more expensive and uncompetitive. A VAT-registered business is required by law to quote its VAT registration number on its invoices.

Transactions may be divided into three broad categories to determine their liability to VAT:

1. Outside the scope of VAT.

2. Exempt.

3. Taxable.
    (a) zero-rated;
    (b) lower rate;
    (c) standard rate.

Factoring of debts

Factoring is a way of getting up-front finance on invoiced sales and this is its main attraction for most of its customers. Depending on the type of service negotiated, the factoring company may also maintain the sales ledger, operate credit control procedures, take the bad debt risk and offer informal advice and support. For convenience, factoring services may be divided into three broad categories, namely: non-recourse factoring; recourse factoring; and invoice discounting.

Non-recourse factoring

The factoring company will advance up to about 85 per cent of invoices issued to approved customers. This can normally be done within 24 hours of the issue of the invoice and the factoring company takes the bad debt risk. It will, of course, take over the rights against the customer and it is insuring against non-payment not slow payment.

The existence of factoring is usually disclosed to the customer, who is asked to pay directly to the factoring company. When this is done, the factoring company will deduct its fees, then forward the percentage of the invoice not originally advanced. The factoring company will maintain the sales ledger, send out statements and operate credit control procedures.

It is normal for the existence of factoring to be disclosed to the customer. However, some factoring companies offer a service where this does not happen. If factoring is not disclosed, the factoring company does not send out statements and does not operate credit control procedures. If factoring is not disclosed, the customer will pay the business issuing the invoice. The appropriate sum must then be forwarded to the factoring company.

Recourse factoring

This operates in the same way as non-recourse factoring, but the factoring company does not take the bad debt risk. For this reason it is likely to be cheaper. A specified time is agreed and if payment has not been received by the due date, then the client must reimburse the factor with the amount advanced.

Invoice discounting

The working of invoice discounting is best illustrated with an example. Let us suppose that your sales ledger totals £1 million. The factoring company will take a legal charge over all the debts, then write a cheque for say 80 per cent (£800,000). You will pay interest and a fee, but so long as the total sales ledger stays at £1 million no further advance will be made.

If at the end of a month the total sales ledger balance has grown to £1,200,000 the factoring company will advance a further £160,000 (80 per cent x £200,000). If at the end of the following month the total sales ledger balance has dropped to £900,000 you must pay £240,000 to the factoring company (80 per cent x £300,000). This series of monthly adjustments will continue until the arrangement is terminated, when the whole outstanding balance must be repaid.

Factoring is available only for business-to-business debts, and not for consumer debts.

Questions to test your understanding

1. A company is wound up and its creditors total £400,000. There are £500,000 preference shares and £500,000 ordinary shares. Net assets are £700,000. How much money will the ordinary shareholders get?

2. A bank overdraft is secured by a debenture and is repayable on demand. The bank demands repayment at 10.00 a.m. on 8 February. When is repayment due?

3. An employee has a PAYE tax code of 317L. How much may he earn in a tax year before income tax is deducted?

4. What class of national insurance contributions is payable by employees?

5. Is VAT a direct or an indirect tax?

6. In the case of non-recourse factoring, does the factoring company take the bad debt risk?

INSTANT TIP

You should manage taxes efficiently and you must obey the law, but money saved by legitimately paying less tax is just as valuable as money saved in other ways.

Answers to questions asked in this book

Chapter 1

1. Different types of account

1. Stock account

Asset account
Balance sheet
Debit balance

2. Rental income account

Income account
Profit and loss account
Credit balance

3. Bank overdraft account

Liability account
Balance sheet
Credit balance

4. Wages account

Expenditure account
Profit and loss account
Debit balance

5. Share capital account
Capital account
Balance sheet
Credit balance

6. Revenue reserves account
Capital account
Balance sheet
Credit balance

7. Invoiced sales account

Income account
Profit and loss account
Credit balance

8. Purchase ledger creditors account
Liability account
Balance sheet
Credit balance

9. Trade debtors account

Asset account
Balance sheet
Debit balance

10. Electricity account

Expenditure account
Profit and loss account
Debit balance

2. Accruals and prepayments

Accrual

Interest	£5,000
Invoices	£80,000
	£85,000

Prepayment

Rent	£100,000

3. Depreciation

Plant and machinery	£10,000
Motor vehicles	£10,000
	£20,000

4. Reserves and provisions

100% × £50,000	=	£50,000
2% × £950,000	=	£19,000
		£69,000

Chapter 2

1. A simple profit statement

Henry Smith
Profit Statement for the three months to 31 July

	£	£
Commission received		
Northern region	4,300	
Southern region	4,200	
		8,500
Less expenses		
Advertising	1,800	
Bank charges	50	
Interest	230	
Leaflets	390	
Miscellaneous expenses	710	
Office costs	1,170	
Other motor expenses	690	
Petrol	1,720	
Postage	440	
Property costs	850	
Telephone	330	
		8,380
Net profit before tax		120

2. Profit statement for a trading company

ABC Trading
Profit Statement for the six months to 31 December

	£	£
Sales		300,000
Stock at 30 June	120,000	
Add purchases in period	220,000	
	340,000	
Less stock at 31 December	90,200	
		249,800
Gross profit		50,200
Less overheads		31,600
Net profit before tax		18,600
Less tax		4,650
Net profit after tax		13,950

3. A balance sheet

Laslo Tamasi
Balance sheet at 30 April

	£	£
Fixed assets		
Leasehold property	100,000	
Plant and machinery	140,000	
Motor vehicles	30,000	
		270,000
Current assets		
Stock	150,000	
Trade debtors	160,000	
Bank	10,000	
	320,000	

Less current liabilities

Trade creditors	200,000	
Taxation	80,000	
	280,000	

Net current assets		40,000
		310,000

Capital

Capital reserve	70,000	
Revenue reserve	240,000	
		310,000

Chapter 3

1. Yes.
2. No – but they almost always do. If they do not, the directors must disclose the fact and give their reasons.
3. Yes.
4. No – debts due in up to one year must be shown separately from debts due after one year.
5. Yes.
6. Not if it is made on fully commercial terms. At the time of publication this is a matter of some political controversy and it is possible that changes to the law could result.
7. It is a cash outflow of £35,000.

Chapter 4

Dracula Dogfoods
Cash flow forecast for half year

	January £000	February £000	March £000	April £000	May £000	June £000
Receipts						
Customers	700	500	530	490	736	811
Government grant	–	–	70	–	–	–
All other income	30	30	30	30	30	30
	730	530	630	520	766	841
Payments						
Salaries and bonuses	60	60	60	60	150	60
Tax	–	–	–	–	–	134
Capital expenditure	20	60	20	20	20	20
Interest	8	8	7	6	6	5
Creditors	612	330	340	418	421	607
All other expenditure	40	40	40	40	40	20
	740	498	467	544	637	846
Excess of receipts over payments	(10)	32	163	(24)	129	(5)
Add opening bank balance	(768)	(778)	(746)	(583)	(607)	(478)
Closing bank balance	(778)	(746)	(583)	(607)	(478)	(483)

Chapter 5

1. $\dfrac{2{,}254{,}000}{11{,}550{,}000}$ = 19.5%

2. 6,231,000 to 11,550,000 which is 0.54 to 1

3. 2,254,000 to 1,133,000 = 2.0 times

4. The dividend per share is $\dfrac{1{,}133{,}000}{5{,}900{,}000}$ = 19.2 pence

The dividend yield is $\dfrac{19.2}{525.0}$ = 3.7%

5. $\dfrac{2{,}254{,}000}{5{,}900{,}000}$ = 38.2 pence

6. $\dfrac{2{,}254{,}000}{44{,}166{,}000}$ = 5.1%

7. $\dfrac{4{,}479{,}000}{1{,}664{,}000}$ = 2.7 times

8. $\dfrac{26{,}928{,}000}{3{,}659{,}000}$ = 7.4 times

9. £2,648,000 less £3,659,000 = £1,011,000 negative

10. $\dfrac{9{,}177{,}000}{44{,}166{,}000} \times 365$ = 75.8 days

11. $\dfrac{5{,}188{,}000}{32{,}400{,}000} \times 365$ = 58.4 days

Chapter 6

1. Payback

	Saving £	Period
Year 1	12,000	12 months
Year 2	12,000	12 months
Year 3	12,000	12 months
Year 4	4,000	4 months
	40,000	40 months

2. Return on investment (using the average profits method)

Additional profits before depreciation

	£
Year 1	12,000
Year 2	12,000
Year 3	12,000
Year 4	12,000
Year 5	12,000
	60,000
Less depreciation	34,000
Profit after depreciation	26,000

Average profit per year is $\dfrac{26,000}{5}$ = £5,200

Average investment

	£
Initial investment	40,000
Less residual value	6,000
	34,000

Average investment is $\dfrac{34,000}{2}$ = £17,000

Return on investment is $\dfrac{5,200 \times 100}{17,000}$ = 30.6%

3. Discounted cash flow

Year 1
£12,000 × 0.9   = £10,800

Year 2
£12,000 × 0.9 × 0.9   = £9,720

Year 3
£12,000 × 0.9 × 0.9 × 0.9   = £8,748

Year 4
£12,000 × 0.9 × 0.9 × 0.9 × 0.9   = £7,873

Year 5
£18,000 × 0.9 × 0.9 × 0.9 × 0.9 × 0.9   = £10,628

Summary

	£	£
Expenditure		40,000
Year 1 discounted saving	10,800	
Year 2 discounted saving	9,720	
Year 3 discounted saving	8,748	
Year 4 discounted saving	7,873	
Year 5 discounted saving	10,628	
		47,769
Net saving discounted to present value		**(7,769)**

Chapter 8

1.

Salzburg Airlines
April cost statement

	Budapest $	Warsaw $	Total $
Revenue	300,000	430,000	730,000
Costs			
Direct	110,000	160,000	270,000
Indirect	160,000	200,000	360,000
	270,000	360,000	630,000
Profit	30,000	70,000	100,000

If the Budapest route was to be shut down and if indirect costs were not cut, the position would be as follows:

	$
Revenue	430,000
Costs	
Direct	160,000
Indirect	360,000
	520,000
Loss	(90,000)

2.

1. Price variance

	£
Standard price (3,000 kilometres × £0.80)	2,400
Actual price	2,500
Favourable variance	100

2. Driver's cost variance

	£
Standard cost (3,000 kilometres × £0.40)	1,200
Actual cost	1,300
Unfavourable variance	(100)

3. Vehicle costs variance

	£
Standard cost (3,000 kilometres × £0.20)	600
Actual cost	700
Unfavourable variance	(100)

3.

	£	Unit basis £
Sales (61,000 units)	305,000	5.00
Less variable costs	101,666	1.66
Contribution	203,334	3.34
Less fixed costs	150,000	2.46
Net profit	53,334	0.88

4.

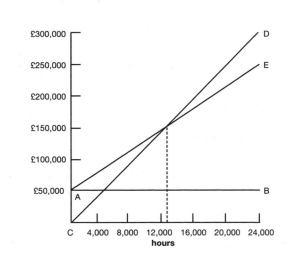

Line A – B is the fixed costs of £50,000
Line C – D is the revenue of £12 per hour
Line A – E is the variable costs of £8 per hour

The break-even point is 12,500 hours, as follows:

	£
Revenue (12,500 x £12)	150,000
Costs	
Fixed	50,000
Variable (12,500 x £8)	100,000
	150,000

13,500 hours must be charged for the business to make a profit of £4,000.

Once the break-even point has been reached every extra hour charged gives £4 profit. So 1,000 extra hours will result in £4,000 extra profit.

Chapter 9

1. Rescue the company as a going concern.
2. No – only with the permission of the court or the agreement of the administrator.
3. Yes.
4. £800.

Chapter 10

1. It depends on the rights of the preference shareholders, but the ordinary shareholders will probably receive nothing.
2. 10.00 a.m. on 8 February.
3. 3,170.
4. Class 1 contributions.
5. An indirect tax
6. Yes.

Index

UNIVERSITY OF LINCOLN